Stench of Kerosene

and other short short stories

selected by

Steve Bowles

The right of the University of Cambridge to print and sell all manner of books was granted by Henry VIII in 1534. The University has printed and published continuously since 1584.

Cambridge University Press

Cambridge New York
Port Chester Melbourne Sydney

Published by the Press Syndicate of the University of Cambridge
The Pitt Building, Trumpington Street, Cambridge CB2 1RP
40 West 20th Street, New York, NY 10011–4211, USA
10 Stamford Road, Oakleigh, Melbourne 3166, Australia

First published 1991

Printed in Great Britain by the University Press, Cambridge

British Library cataloguing-in-publication data
Stench of Kerosene.
I. Bowles, Steve
823'.914 [F]
ISBN 0 521 39579 8

Acknowledgements

The author and publisher would like to thank the following for their kind permission to reproduce stories in this book:

'A Rat and Some Renovations' by Bernard MacLaverty reprinted by permission of The Blackstaff Press; 'The Red Shoes' by Julie Hollings reprinted by kind permission of the author and her agent Anthony Brandt; 'Being a Girl' from *Taking the Chook* by Jean Holkner reprinted by permission of the author and Penguin Books Australia Ltd; 'Who Shall Dwell' by H C Neal was taken from *Playboy Book of Science Fiction and Fantasy* and 'Hobbyist' by Frederic Brown was taken from *Playboy Book of Crime and Suspense* – originally appeared in *Playboy* magazine; 'Do You Want My Opinion?' by M E Kerr and 'An Ordinary Woman' by Bette Greene from *Sixteen* edited by Donald Gallo reprinted by permission of HarperCollins Publishers; 'The Happiest Day of Your Life' by Bob Shaw, Doubleday. Copyright © 1970 by The Condé Nast Publications, Inc.; 'Well, Well, Well' by Kate Hall from *A Girl's Best Friend* and 'The Watcher' by J California Cooper from *Homemade Love* reprinted by permission of The Women's Press; 'The Toy Girl' by Paula Clark from *True to Life*, 'The Headache' by Ann Hunter from *Everyday Matters*, and Shopping for One by Anne Cassidy and 'Til Death Us Do Part' by Jacqueline Brine from *Everyday Matters 2* reprinted by permission of Sheba Feminist Publishers; 'Slipper Satin' by Alex La Guma reprinted by permission of the Tessa Sayle Agency; 'The Dead Woman' by Sarah Baylis from *Storia 1* reprinted by permission of Richard Scott Simon © Sarah Baylis Estate 1988; 'Fatal Woman' from *Night-side* by Joyce Carol Oates (Victor Gollancz Ltd) reprinted by permission of Murray Pollinger; 'Uncle Ifor's Welsh Dresser' by Pat Lacey reprinted by kind permission of the author; 'Stench of Kerosene' by Amrita Pritam reprinted by kind permission of Jaico Publishing House, 121–125 Mahatma Ghandi Road, Bombay, India; 'Another Evening at the Club' by Alifa Rifaat, translated by Denys Johnson-Davies reprinted by permission of Quartet Books Limited; 'Sunday in the Park' by Bel Kaufman reprinted from *The Available Press/PEN Short Story Collection* (New York, Ballantine, 1985) by permission of the author; 'The Shelter' from *Under the Banyan Tree* by R K Narayan reprinted by permission of William Heinemann Limited; 'The Unseeing Eye' by Hanan Al-Shaykh reprinted by kind permission of the author; 'Faces' from *The Shirt From A Hanged Man's Back* by Dennis Hamley (1984) reprinted by permission of Andre Deutsch Ltd; 'The Hitch-hiker' from *The Bite and Other Apocryphal Tales* by Francis Greig © 1981 by Francis Greig, reprinted by permission of Jonathan Clowes Ltd, London on behalf of Francis Greig; 'Doctor's Orders' by John Suter from *Stories To Stay Awake By* by Alfred Hitchcock reprinted by permission of Random House Inc; 'Mr Lupescu' by Anthony Boucher reprinted by permission of Curtis Brown Ltd. Copyright 1945 by Weird Tales Magazine. Copyright © renewed 1972 by Phyllis White; 'Hobo' by Robert Bloch reprinted by kind permission of The Pimlico Agency Inc; 'The Wasteland' from *Debbie Go Home* by Alan Paton (Jonathan Cape) reprinted by permission of Random Century Group and the Estate of Alan Paton; 'You Are Now Entering the Human Heart' by Janet Frame reprinted by permission of Curtis Brown Ltd. Copyright © Janet Frame 1983.

Every effort has been made to reach all the copyright holders; the publishers would be glad to hear from anyone whose rights have been unknowingly infringed.

We would also like to thank the Jaico Publishing House for allowing us to use 'Stench of Kerosene' as the title for this collection.

Cover illustration by Ian Parratt.

GO

Contents

Fear

Introduction

The choice of stories for this collection has been guided by a desire to find short pieces which allow maximum flexibility when the book is used in schools. I've imagined an audience of secondary school pupils and have looked for stories which aren't, to my knowledge, widely available in stock cupboards already. Consequently, I've avoided over-anthologised pieces like Asimov's *The Fun They Had*, Bradbury's *The Pedestrian* (etc.) or Greene's *I Spy* and *The Case for the Defence*. Likewise, I've deliberately omitted standard authors like Saki, Leacock, Thurber and O'Flaherty.

The arrangement of the stories in any anthology is always open to criticism and I hope that the thematic contents list will not prove restrictive when the stories are used. They could have been organised in many ways. Some people might prefer to look at *Another Evening at the Club* or *'Til Death Us Do Part* alongside other stories which deal with fear. *Slipper Satin* and *The Wasteland* both illustrate the evils of apartheid, one overtly, through personal tragedy, one through implication and symbolism, and they could, of course, be read with other stories from South Africa. *The Happiest Day of Your Life* and *The Dead Woman* both have things to say about decisions which affect children. The categories used on the Contents page are, therefore, to a large extent arbitrary and these notes are intended to sketch other ways of linking the stories as well as to indicate other writing which might be read alongside the pieces included.

One particularly interesting principle for organising short stories in an anthology was suggested by James Moffett and Kenneth McElheny in their collection *Points of View* (Mentor). Stories there are grouped according to their narrative style – diary narration, dramatic monologue, subjective narration, detached autobiography and so on. Such an approach would need to be modified for British schools but there might be very good reasons for linking, say, stories with twist endings like *Who Shall Dwell?*, *Mr Lupescu* and *Well, Well, Well* in order to show different methods of creating these endings: using the preconceptions of the reader, limiting the field of vision by cutting out description, setting up expectations of an ending which doesn't arrive . . . By extending the range of stories examined (e.g. *Hobo, The Hitch-hiker, Faces*) discussion might range over why some twist endings work and some don't. Twist endings could be compared for effectiveness with the 'pregnant' final paragraphs of stories like *Slipper Satin* or *A Respectable Woman,* where the full significance of the conclusions sometimes escapes less sophisticated readers. The difficulty of ending stories which have the feel of personal anecdotes might arise here, too: why does *The Red Shoes* close in a more satisfying way than either *Being a Girl* or *A Rat and Some Renovations*?

Comparing narrative styles could also lead to very different groupings from those arising from thematic arrangement. (How do the 'facts' of the story reach the reader in *The Red Shoes, The Toy Girl, Fatal Woman* and *You Are Now Entering the Human Heart*? What does the writer feel about the central character in each of these stories and how do you know?) Sometimes, however, a singled-minded focus on narrative style can result in the selection of stories which are interesting structurally but which lack a powerful punch. Other brilliant stories are just too long for this particular collection (e.g. Daniel Keyes' *Flowers for Algernon*). No single anthology can include every short story which deserves a place in schools; no arrangement of stories in a collection will meet with the approval of every reader. I hope that the list of further reading – a highly selective one – will be helpful to anyone who wants to follow up some of the ideas I've tried to sketch here. For more detailed suggestions of individual stories to investigate, please contact me via the Senior Editor, English and Drama, at Cambridge University Press.

Further Reading

Other collections of short short stories

Isaac Asimov, Martin Greenberg and Joseph Olander (eds.), *100 Great Science Fiction Short Short Stories* (Robson)
Roy Blatchford (ed.), *Shorties* (Unwin Hyman)
Robert Shapard and James Thomas (eds.), *Sudden Fiction* (Penguin)
Arnold Thompson (ed.), *Storylines* (Hodder & Stoughton Educational)

Other collections which include short short stories

Steve Bowles (ed.), *A Question of Blood* (Collins Educational)
Steve Bowles (ed.), *Twisters* (Fontana Teen Tracks)
Philip Boys and Corinne Pearlman (eds.), *The Comic Book of First Love* (Virago Upstarts)
Jan Bradshaw and Mary Hemming (eds.), *Girls Next Door* (Women's Press)
Paul Jennings, *Unreal* (Puffin)
Paul Jennings, *Unbelievable* (Puffin)
Paul Jennings, *Quirky Tails* (Puffin)
Nick Jones (ed.), *Contemporary Stories 1* (Oxford)
Nick Jones (ed.), *Contemporary Stories 2* (Oxford)
Trevor Millum (ed.), *Pigs Is Pigs* (Unwin Hyman)
John Seely, Frank Green and Graham Nutbrown (eds.), *From the Top Deck and other stories* (Oxford)

The above anthologies contain stories which cover a wide range of narrative styles and provide plenty of material to supplement the stories in this book if they were to be used as a basis for investigating short story structure. They also include stories at all levels of difficulty.

Anyone wishing to follow up the idea of re-writing old stories, as exemplified by *The Hitch-hiker* and *Facco*, might find the following books useful.

Jan Harold Brunvand, *The Vanishing Hitch-hiker: Urban Legends and their Meanings* (Picador)
Francis Greig, *The Bite and other apocryphal tales* (Cape)
Paul Smith, *The Book of Nasty Legends / The Book of Nastier Legends* (Routledge & Kegan Paul)

A Rat and Some Renovations

Bernard MacLaverty

Almost everyone in Ireland must have experienced American visitors or, as we called them, 'The Yanks'. Just before we were visited for the first time, my mother decided to have the working kitchen modernised. We lived in a terrace of dilapidated Victorian houses whose front gardens measured two feet by the breadth of the house. The scullery, separated from the kitchen by a wall, was the same size as the garden, and just as arable. When we pulled out the vegetable cupboard we found three or four potatoes which had fallen down behind and taken root. Ma said, 'God, if the Yanks had seen that.'

She engaged the workmen early so the job would be finished and the newness worn off by the time the Yanks arrived. She said she wouldn't like them to think that she got it done up just for them.

The first day the workmen arrived they demolished the wall, ripped up the floor and left the cold water tap hanging four feet above a bucket. We didn't see them again for three weeks. Grandma kept trying to make excuses for them, saying that it was very strenuous work. My mother however managed to get them back and they worked for three days, erecting a sink unit and leaving a hole for the outlet pipe. It must have been through this hole that the rat got in.

The first signs were discovered by Ma in the drawer of the new unit. She called me and said, 'What's those?' I looked and saw six hard brown ovals trundling about the drawer.

'Ratshit,' I said. Ma backed disbelievingly away, her hands over her mouth, repeating, 'It's mouse, it's mouse, it must be mouse.'

The man from next door, a Mr Frank Twoomey, who had lived most of his life in the country, was called – he said from the size of them, it could well be a horse. At this my mother took her nightdress and toothbrush and moved in with an aunt across the street, leaving the brother and myself with the problem. Armed with a hatchet and shovel we banged and brattled the cupboards, then when we felt sure it was gone we blocked the hole with hardboard and sent word to Ma to return, that all was well.

It was after two days safety that she discovered the small brown bombs again. I met her with her nightdress under her arm, in the path. She just said, 'I found more,' and headed for her sister's.

That evening it was Grandma's suggestion that we should borrow the Grimleys' cat. The brother was sent and had to pull it from beneath the side-board because it was very shy of strangers. He carried it across the road and the rat-killer was so terrified of the traffic and Peter squeezing it that it peed all down his front. By this time Ma's curiosity had got the better of her and she ventured from her sister's to stand pale and nervous in our path. The brother set the cat down and turned to look for a cloth to wipe himself. The cat shot past him down the hall, past Ma who screamed, 'Jesus, the rat', and leapt into the hedge. The cat ran until a bus stopped it with a thud. The Grimleys haven't spoken to us since.

Ma had begun to despair. 'What age do rats live to?' she asked. 'And what'll we do if it's still here when the Yanks come?' Peter said that they loved pigs in the kitchen.

The next day we bought stuff, pungent like phosphorus and spread it on cubes of bread. The idea of this stuff was to roast the rat inside when he ate it so that he would drink himself to death.

'Just like Uncle Matt,' said Peter. He tactlessly read out the instructions to Grandma who then came out in sympathy with the rat. Ma thought it may have gone outside, so to make sure, we littered the yard with pieces of bread as well. In case it didn't work Ma decided to do a novena of masses so she got up the next morning and on the driveway to the chapel which runs along the back of our house she noticed six birds with their feet in the air, stone dead.

Later that day the rat was found in the same condition on the kitchen floor. It was quickly buried in the dust-bin using the shovel as a hearse. The next day the workmen came, finished the job, and the Yanks arrived just as the paint was drying.

They looked strangely out of place with their brown, leathery faces, rimless glasses and hat brims flamboyantly large, as we met them at the boat . . . Too summery by half, against the dripping eaves of the sheds at the dock-yard. At home by a roaring fire on a July day, after having laughed a little at the quaintness of the taxi, they exchanged greetings, talked about family likenesses, jobs, and then dried up. For the next half hour the conversation had to be manufactured, except for a comparison of education systems which was confusing and therefore lasted longer. Then everything stopped.

The brother said, 'I wouldn't call this an embarrassing silence.'

They all laughed, nervously dispelling the silence but not the embarrassment.

Ma tried to cover up. 'Would yous like another cup of cawfee?' Already she had begun to pick up the accent. They agreed and the oldish one with the blue hair followed her out to the kitchen.

'Gee, isn't this madern,' she said.

Ma, untacking her hand from the paint on the drawer, said, 'Yeah, we done it up last year.'

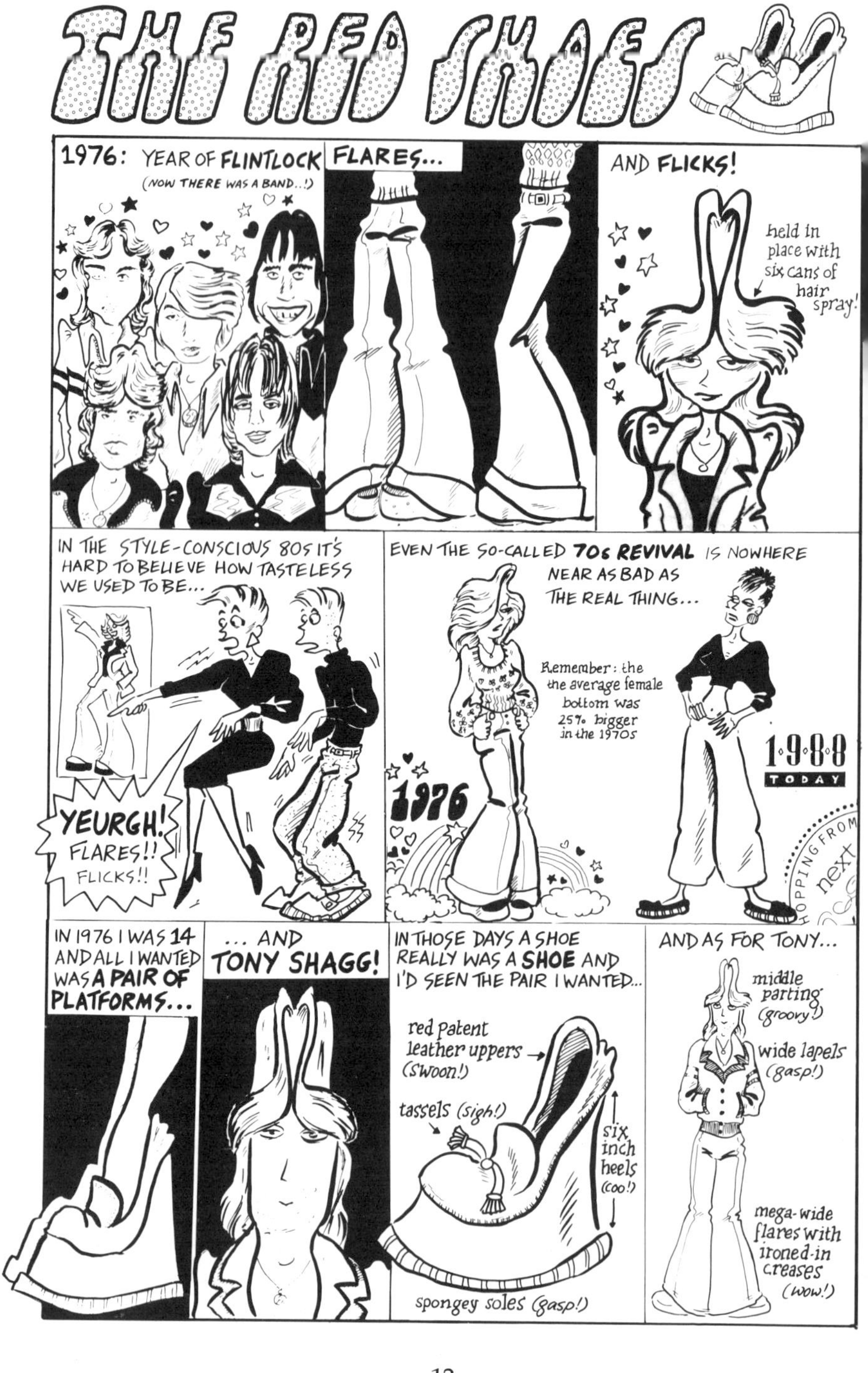
THE RED SHOES
1976: YEAR OF FLINTLOCK
(NOW THERE WAS A BAND...!)
FLARES...
AND FLICKS!
held in place with six cans of hair spray!
IN THE STYLE-CONSCIOUS 80s IT'S HARD TO BELIEVE HOW TASTELESS WE USED TO BE...
YEURGH! FLARES!! FLICKS!!
EVEN THE SO-CALLED 70s REVIVAL IS NOWHERE NEAR AS BAD AS THE REAL THING...
Remember: the the average female bottom was 25% bigger in the 1970s
1976
1988
TODAY
HOPPING FROM
next
IN 1976 I WAS 14 AND ALL I WANTED WAS A PAIR OF PLATFORMS...
... AND TONY SHAGG!
IN THOSE DAYS A SHOE REALLY WAS A SHOE AND I'D SEEN THE PAIR I WANTED...
red patent leather uppers (swoon!)
tassels (sigh!)
six inch heels (coo!)
spongey soles (gasp!)
AND AS FOR TONY...
middle parting (groovy!)
wide lapels (gasp!)
mega-wide flares with ironed-in creases (wow!)

EVERY DAY, ON THE WAY HOME FROM SCHOOL, I'D STOP AND LOOK AT THE SHOES. I REALLY **LOVED THEM!**
I KNEW TONY WOULD **LOVE** THEM TOO. I'D SEEN THE LOOK IN HIS EYES WHEN HE SAW A REALLY **HIGH PLATFORM...**
WHO IS THAT WALLY?
PRAT!
MY PARENTS HAD THEIR DOUBTS...
YOU'LL BREAK YOUR NECK!
AW MUM!
THE KILLER SHOES
THE DAILY SCUM
NO NEWS! BUT LOTS OF TRINGO ZINGO BINGO!
WOMAN FALLS TO DEATH FROM PLATFOR SHOES!
"THEY WRECK LIVES" CLAIMS BISHOP!
OVER 2FT HIGH!
I BLAME THE INNER SOLES SAYS HUBBY
CONT'D ON BACK
RUNAWAY LOVE
HUH! I BET THEY'RE NOT **SCHOOL REGULATION!** WHAT'S WRONG WITH YOUR SCHOOL SHOES ANYWAY?
WHAT WAS WRONG! THEY WERE **FLAT**!!
TONY WOULD **NEVER** FANCY ME IN MY SCHOOL SHOES...
COR! ANDY - I MET THIS **BIRD**, RIGHT, AND HER **PLATFORMS**, RIGHT, THEY WERE AT LEAST **EIGHT INCHES**... AND CORK, TOO!

I WAS DETERMINED TO EARN THE MONEY FOR THE SHOES
MUM - I WASHED YOUR SILK SUIT - WORTH A FIVER, 'EH?
SLADE
GASP IT'S RUINED!
DAD - I THREW OUT ALL THOSE FUNNY OLD SMUTTY MAGAZINES YOU KEPT IN THE SHED - HOW MUCH DO I GET?
THE CHILD'S A RETARD!
HERE - TAKE THE MONEY JUST DON'T DO ANY MORE JOBS!
TA DAD!
AT THE SHOE SHOP...
STOMP SHOES
SALE
PRICES SLASHED!
HALF PRICE!!
A SALE! FAB!
I SLEPT OUTSIDE THE SHOP FOR FIVE DAYS BEFORE THE SALE BEGAN...
STOMP SHOES
SALE
PRICES SLASHED
ON THE FIFTH DAY THE FIGHT WAS FIERCE...
HALF PRICE!!
GOTCHA!
CLUNK!
BUT IT WAS WORTH IT!!

THAT NIGHT I WORE THE SHOES TO THE DISCO...
SHANG-A-LANG-A-LANG
I COULD FEEL TONY'S EYES ON ME...
SHA-LA LA!
WHEN I SAT DOWN...
HI, MICHELLE, CAN I JOIN YOU?
ER... I'LL GO AND POWDER MY NOSE!
YOU LOOKED FAB ON THE DANCEFLOOR, 'CHELLE... THOSE SHOES...
SOON IT WAS TIME TO LEAVE...
CAN I WALK YOU HOME?

BUT WHEN WE STOOD UP TO LEAVE...
'ERE, YOU'RE TALLER THAN ME!!
I CAN'T GO OUT WITH A BIRD THAT'S TALLER THAN ME! YOU CAN'T WEAR THOSE SHOES IF YOU'RE GONNA BE MY BIRD!
GRRR!
IT WAS HARD BUT NOT THAT HARD...
GOODBYE THEN TONY!
UH?
THERE ARE PLENTY MORE LIKE TONY IN THE WORLD
BUT THOSE SHOES WERE MY FIRST LOVE!!
THE END
Julie Hollings '88

Being a Girl

Jean Holkner

'Why can't you be like other girls?' was my mother's continual despairing cry.

You could hardly blame her.

As a girl I was a complete failure.

By the time I was fourteen I was five foot six, making it highly improbable that I would ever find a Jewish boy I could look up to.

There wasn't much my mother could do about this, except perhaps bitterly regret having married my father who was five foot ten and the cause of it all.

As well as my size there was the problem of my face.

'I never had so many pimples when I was a young girl,' said my mother and dragged me off to the Children's Hospital.

'I'm sorry,' said the Sister. 'We don't treat anyone over seventeen here.'

'But she's only fourteen,' pleaded my mother.

'Really?' said Sister, looking up at me interestedly. 'Well fill in this form and wait over there.'

After a couple of hours of sliding along the benches it was finally our turn.

Dr Newman was very young – I was probably his first important case.

He listened to my mother describing the sudden advent of my pimples. 'Has she – er – got her period yet?' he asked, looking down at the floor.

'Of course,' replied my mother proudly. 'On the tenth of August last year.'

It was my turn to look down at the floor.

'Has she got any pubic hair?' asked the doctor writing very busily on my card.

'Pardon?' asked my mother.

'Doesn't matter,' mumbled the doctor. 'Has she got any hair under her armpits?'

'No,' I said indignantly before my mother could give away any more of my secrets.

'Well,' he said scribbling furiously, 'I wouldn't worry too much – these things usually clear themselves up when – er – it's time. Get some of this cream from the chemist.' And he ushered us thankfully to the door.

After that my mother decided that if I couldn't be beautiful I'd better learn to be useful.

So I ironed the family hankies till they turned deep brown, broke nearly as many plates as I dried and once even emptied the remains of the chicken soup down the sink mistaking it for dishwater.

'Why do you just stand there watching the milk boil over?' my mother asked sorrowfully one breakfast time.

I didn't know what to say. I could hardly tell her I'd been dancing under a tropical moon with the boy of my dreams.

When cooking classes started at school my mother wasn't as pleased as she might have been.

'What are they going to teach you there?' she said. 'How to roast a pork – God forbid – or to make oysters?'

On the first day of cooking my mother's fears were put to rest.

'Basic cooking is what we will learn here,' said Miss Bakewell. 'Stews, puddings, bread and cakes. You will each bring fourpence every week and whatever you cook will be your lunch. You will work in pairs.'

So Annie and I gravitated towards each other – a partnership which produced many a culinary disaster.

One of our first tasks was to go shopping for the ingredients for a fruit cake.

'You will bring back two pounds of mixed fruit,' said Miss Bakewell to Annie and me.

So we brought back three apples, two oranges and a

banana. It took us a while to work out why everyone laughed.

Except Miss Bakewell of course. She had a rough time of it that year. Whenever the class was cooking a meat dish, Annie, Frieda Finkle and I would form a deputation to remind her that we weren't allowed to eat any non-Jewish meat.

So we were appointed 'housekeepers' for that day which meant we polished the silver, set the table and slid down the banisters which was our way of dusting them.

We made ourselves pretty unpopular with the rest of the class who had to cook things called Shepherd's Pie and Irish Stew and then struggle to eat them or throw them in the bin when Miss Bakewell wasn't looking.

We Chosen Ones made do very nicely with the dessert of the day, usually custard pudding or junket, along with lots of fresh bread and butter.

One day Miss Bakewell announced that we were now advanced enough to make our own bread.

Annie took it upon herself to mix the dough so I stole away quietly to the window and looked out on the street while working out that there were still seven cooking days before the end of term.

'Now girls,' Miss Bakewell was saying when I sneaked back to my bench-top, 'don't forget to put a tea-towel on your bread while it is rising.'

Annie was by now nowhere to be seen. I guessed she'd gone to the lavatory where she would spend the next quarter of an hour combing her hair down over one eye like her favourite film star, Veronica Lake.

I picked up the tray with the dough on it and put it in the oven, tea-towel and all.

After a few minutes a strange smell began to fill the air.

'What's that burning?' cried Miss Bakewell and she rushed towards my oven.

Bravely she flung open the door and out poured smoke, flame and the tattered remains of an Education Department tea towel.

'What am I going to do with you?' groaned my mother that evening as she counted out three shillings and sixpence for a new towel. What she was thinking of course was, 'Where am I ever going to find anyone to marry you?'

But she battled on grimly, trying to make me into a real girl. Once she put me in charge of polishing the floors.

'When I come back,' she said, 'I want to see this lino shining brightly.'

As soon as she was out of sight Lily and I tied the polishing cloths around our feet and skated up and down the passage pretending we were world-famous ice-skaters.

When my mother came back she looked at the fifteen-foot streaks we'd made and sighed deeply.

But she was a forgiving person and when it was time to start knitting at school she nobly came to my rescue.

'Did you knit all these yourself?' asked Miss Woolman suspiciously, examining my scarf, tea-cosy and baby's singlet.

'Oh yes, Miss,' I replied with my fingers crossed behind my back. But I don't think she believed me because much to my mother's indignation all she got for knitting that year was 7½ out of 10.

I didn't do any better at sewing.

'Now girls,' said Miss Singer, 'all you have to do is to pin, tack and hem your square of cotton neatly. With tiny stitches all going the same way of course.'

'Of course'? What did she mean 'of course'?

By the time I'd unpicked my stitches, all of different sizes and all leaning in different directions, three times, Miss Singer and I were both exhausted. Not to mention my square of cotton.

I think my mother finally gave up on the day I did the washing. It was a Sunday and I was alone in the house. 'Why should my mother have to slave over a hot copper all day tomorrow?' I thought.

It was this noble sentiment that held me up throughout the afternoon as I filled the copper with dirty laundry and cold water to cover, threw a lighted piece of newspaper underneath, and got out of the way as fast as possible in case of an explosion.

By the time my mother came in I was stirring the washing with a wooden stick, just like I'd seen her do.

For a moment she just stood there watching it all boiling away merrily – white sheets, coloured jumpers, everybody's underwear. Suddenly my Dad's best red silk socks simmered into view.

With an anguished cry my mother lunged forward in a desperate effort to save them.

All she got for her trouble was a nasty burn.

Later that evening I stood watching her change the dressing on her injured fingers.

'When I grow up,' I said, 'I'm going to be a lawyer and make enough money to have a full-time housekeeper.'

My mother didn't even look up. 'I think that's a very good idea,' she said, and went on bandaging her finger.

Who Shall Dwell?

H.C. Neal

It came on a Sunday afternoon and that was good, because if it had happened on a weekday the father would have been at work and the children at school, leaving the mother at home alone and the whole family disorganised with hardly any hope at all. They had prayed that it would never come, ever, but suddenly here it was.

The father, a slender, young-old man, slightly stooped from years of labour, was resting on the divan and half-listening to a programme of waltz music on the radio. Mother was in the kitchen preparing a chicken for dinner and the younger boy and girl were in the bedroom drawing crude pictures of familiar barnyard animals on a shared slate. The older boy was in the tack shed out back, saddle-soaping some harnesses.

When the waltz programme was interrupted by an announcer with a routine political appeal, the father rose, tapped the ash from his pipe, and ambled lazily into the kitchen.

'How about joining me in a little glass of wine?' he asked, patting his wife affectionately on the hip.

'If you don't think it would be too crowded,' she replied, smiling easily at their standing jest.

He grinned amiably and reached into the cupboard for the bottle and glasses.

Suddenly the radio message was abruptly cut off. A moment of humming silence. Then, in a voice pregnant with barely controlled excitement, the announcer almost shouted:

'Bomb alert! Bomb alert! Attention! Attention! A salvo of missiles has just been launched across the sea, heading this way. Attention! They are expected to strike within the next sixteen minutes. Sixteen minutes! This is a verified alert! Take cover! Take cover! Keep your radios tuned for further instructions.'

'My God!' the father gasped, dropping the glasses. 'Oh, my God!' His ruggedly handsome face was ashen, puzzled, as though he knew beyond a shadow of doubt that this was real – but still could not quite believe it.

'Get the children,' his wife blurted, then dashed to the door to call the older boy. He stared at her a brief moment, seeing the fear in her pretty face, but something else, too, something divorced from the fear. Defiance. And a loathing for all men involved in the making and dispatch of nuclear weapons.

He wheeled then, and ran to the bedroom. 'Let's go,' he snapped, 'shelter drill!' Despite a belated attempt to tone down the second phrase and make it seem like just another of the many rehearsals they'd had, his voice and bearing galvanised the youngsters into instant action. They leaped from the bed without a word and dashed for the door.

He hustled them through the kitchen to the rear door and sent them scooting to the shelter. As he returned to the bedroom for outer garments for himself and his wife, the older boy came running in.

'This is the hot one, Son,' said his father tersely, 'the real one.' He and the boy stared at each other a long moment, both knowing what must be done and each knowing the other would more than do his share, yet wondering still at the frightening fact that it must be done at all.

'How much time we got, Dad?'

'Not long,' the father replied, glancing at his watch, 'twelve, maybe fourteen minutes.'

The boy disappeared into the front room, going after the flashlight and battery radio. The father stepped to the closet, slid the door open and picked up the flat metal box containing their vital papers, marriage licence, birth certificates, etc. He tossed the box on the bed, then took down his wife's shortcoat and his own hunting jacket. Draping the clothing over his arm, he then picked up the metal box and the big family Bible from the headboard on the bed. Everything else they would need had been stored in the shelter the past several months. He heard his wife approaching and turned as she entered the room.

'Ready, Dear?' she asked.

'Yes, we're ready now,' he replied, 'are the kids gone in?'

'They're all down,' she answered, then added with a faint touch of despairing bewilderment, 'I still can't believe it's real.'

'We've got to believe it,' he said, looking her steadily in the eye, 'we can't afford not to.'

Outside, the day was crisp and clear, typical of early fall. Just right for boating on the river, fishing or bird shooting. A regular peach of a day, he thought, for fleeing underground to escape the awesome hell of a nuclear strike. Who was the writer who had said about atomic weapons, 'Would any self-respecting cannibal toss one into a village of women and children?' He looked at his watch again. Four minutes had elapsed since the first alarm. Twelve minutes, more or less, remained.

Inside the shelter, he dogged the door with its double-strength strap iron bar, and looked around to see that his family was squared away. His wife, wearing her attractive blue print cotton frock (he noticed for the first time), was methodically checking the food supplies, assisted by the older son. The small children had already put their initial fright behind them, as is the nature of youngsters, and were drawing on the slate again in quiet, busy glee.

Now it began. The waiting.

They knew, the man and his wife, that others would come soon, begging and crying to be taken in now that the time was here, now that Armageddon had come screaming toward them, stabbing through the sky on stubbed wings of shining steel.

They had argued the aspects of this when the shelter was abuilding. It was in her mind to share their refuge. 'We can't call ourselves Christians and then deny safety to our friends when the showdown comes,' she contended, 'that isn't what God teaches.'

'That's nothing but religious pap,' he retorted with a degree of anger, 'oatmeal Christianity.' For he was a hard-headed man, an Old Testament man. 'God created the family as the basic unit of society,' he reasoned. 'That should make it plain that a man's primary Christian duty is to protect his family.'

'But don't you see?' she protested, 'we must prepare to purify ourselves . . . to rise above this "mine" thinking and be as God's own son, who said, "Love thy neighbour."'

'No,' he replied with finality, 'I can't buy that.' Then, after a moment's thought while he groped for the words to make her understand the truth which burned in the core of his soul, 'It is my family I must save, no one more. You. These kids. Our friends are like the people of Noah's time: he warned them of the coming flood when he built the ark on God's command. He was ridiculed and scoffed at, just as we have been ridiculed. No,' and here his voice took on a new sad sureness, an air of dismal certainty, 'it is meant that if they don't prepare, they die. I see no need for further argument.' And so, she had reluctantly acquiesced.

With seven minutes left, the first knock rang the shelter door. 'Let us in! For God's sake, man, let us in!'

He recognized the voice. It was his first neighbour down the road toward town.

'No!' shouted the father, 'there is only room for us. Go! Take shelter in your homes. You may yet be spared.'

Again came the pounding. Louder. More urgent.

'You let us in or we'll break down this door!' He wondered, with some concern, if they were actually getting a ram of some sort to batter at the door. He was reasonably certain it would hold. At least as long as it must.

The seconds ticked relentlessly away. Four minutes left.

His wife stared at the door in stricken fascination and moaned slightly. 'Steady, girl,' he said, evenly. The children, having halted their game at the first shouting, looked at him in fearful wonderment. He glared at his watch, ran his hands distraughtly through his hair, and said nothing.

Three minutes left.

At that moment, a woman's cry from the outside pierced him in an utterly vulnerable spot, a place the men could never have touched with their desperate demands. 'If you won't let me in,' she cried, 'please take my baby, my little girl.'

He was stunned by her plea. This he had not anticipated.

What must I do? he asked himself in sheer agony. What man on earth could deny a child the chance to live?

At that point, his wife rose, sobbing, and stepped to the door. Before he could move to stop her, she let down the latch and dashed outside. Instantly a three-year old girl was thrust into the shelter. He hastily fought the door latch on again, then stared at the frightened little newcomer in mute rage, hating her with an abstract hatred for simply being there in his wife's place and knowing he could not turn her out.

He sat down heavily, trying desperately to think. The voices outside grew louder. He glanced at his watch, looked at the faces of his own children a long moment, then rose to his feet. There were two minutes left, and he made his decision. He marvelled now that he had even considered any other choice.

'Son,' he said to the older boy, 'you take care of them.' It was as simple as that.

Unlatching the door, he thrust it open and stepped out. The crowd surged toward him. Blocking the door with his body, he snatched up the two children nearest him, a boy and a girl, and shoved them into the shelter. 'Bar that door,' he shouted to his son, 'and don't open it for at least a week!'

Hearing the latch drop into place, he turned and glanced around at the faces in the crowd. Some of them were still babbling incoherently, utterly panic-stricken. Others were quiet now, resigned, no longer afraid.

Stepping to his wife's side, he took her hand and spoke in a warm, low tone. 'They will be all right, the boy will lead them.' He grinned reassuringly and added, 'We should be together, you and I.'

She smiled wordlessly through her tears and squeezed his hand, exchanging with him in the one brief gesture a lifetime and more of devotion.

Then struck the first bomb, blinding them, burning them, blasting them into eternity. Streaking across the top of the world, across the extreme northern tip of Greenland, then flaming downrange through the chilled Arctic skies, it had passed over Moscow, over Voronezh, and on over Krasny to detonate high above their city of Shakhty.

Do You Want My Opinion?

M.E. Kerr

The night before last I dreamed that Cynthia Slater asked my opinion of *The Catcher in the Rye*.

Last night I dreamed I told Lauren Lake what I thought about John Lennon's music, Picasso's art, and Soviet-American relations.

It's getting worse.

I'm tired of putting my head under the cold-water faucet.

Early this morning my father came into my room and said, 'John, are you getting serious with Eleanor Rossi?'

'Just because I took her out three times?'

'Just because you sit up until all hours of the night talking with her!' he said. 'We know all about it, John. Her mother called your mother.'

I didn't say anything. I finished getting on my socks and shoes.

He was standing over me, ready to deliver the lecture. It always started the same way.

'You're going to get in trouble if you're intimate, John. You're too young to let a girl get a hold on you.'

'Nobody has a hold on me, Dad.'

'Not yet. But one thought leads to another. Before you know it, you'll be exploring all sorts of ideas together, knowing each other so well you'll finish each other's sentences.'

'Okay,' I said. 'Okay.'

'Stick to lovemaking.'

'Right,' I said.

'Don't discuss ideas.'

'Dad,' I said, 'kids today–'

'Not nice kids. Aren't you a nice kid?'

'Yeah, I'm a nice kid.'

'And Eleanor, too?'

'Yeah, Eleanor too.'

'Then show some respect for her. Don't ask her opinions. I know it's you who starts it.'

'Okay,' I said.

'Okay?' he said. He mussed up my hair, gave me a poke in the ribs, and went down to breakfast.

By the time I got downstairs, he'd finished his eggs and was sipping coffee, holding hands with my mother.

I don't think they've exchanged an idea in years.

To tell you the truth, I can't imagine them exchanging ideas, ever, though I know they did. She has a collection of letters he wrote to her on every subject from Shakespeare to Bach, and he treasures this little essay she wrote for him when they were engaged, on her feelings about French drama.

All I've ever seen them do is hug and kiss. Maybe they wait until I'm asleep to get into their discussions. Who knows?

I walked to school with Edna O'Leary.

She's very beautiful. I'll say that for her. We put our arms round each other, held tight, and stopped to kiss along the way. But I'd never ask her opinion on any subject. She just doesn't appeal to me that way.

'I love your eyes, John,' she said.

'I love your smile, Edna.'

'Do you like this colour on me?'

'I like you in blue better.'

'Oh, John, that's interesting, because I like you in blue, too.'

We chatted and kissed and laughed as we went up the winding walk to school.

In the schoolyard everyone was cuddled up except for some of the lovers, who were off walking in pairs, talking. I doubted that they were saying trivial things. Their fingers were pointing and their hands were moving, and they were frowning.

You can always tell the ones in love by their passionate gestures as they get into conversations.

I went into the Boys' room for a smoke.

That's right, I'm starting to smoke. That's the state of mind I'm in.

My father says I'm going through a typical teenage stage, but I don't think he understands how crazy it's making me. He says he went through the same thing, but I just can't picture that.

On the bathroom wall there were heads drawn with kids' initials inside.

There was the usual graffiti:

Josephine Merril is a brain! I'd like to know her opinions!

If you'd like some interesting conversation, try Loulou.

I smoked a cigarette and thought of Lauren Lake.

Who didn't think of Lauren? I made a bet with myself that there were half a dozen guys like me remembering Lauren's answer to Mr Porter's question last week in Thoughts class.

A few more answers like that, and those parents who want Thoughts taken out of the school curriculum will have their way. Some kid will run home and tell the folks what goes on in Porter's room, and Thoughts will be replaced by another course in history, language, body maintenance, sex education, or some other boring subject that isn't supposed to be provocative.

'What are dreams?' Mr Porter asked.

Naturally, Lauren's hand shot up first. She can't help herself.

'Lauren?'

'Dreams can be waking thoughts or sleeping thoughts,' she said. 'I had a dream once, a waking one, about a world where you could say anything on your mind, but you had to be very careful about who you touched. You could ask anyone his opinion, but you couldn't just go up and kiss him.'

Some of the kids got red-faced and sucked in their breaths. Even Porter said, 'Now, take it easy, Lauren. Some of your classmates aren't as advanced as you are.'

One kid yelled out, 'If you had to be careful about touching, how would you reproduce in that world?'

'The same way we do in our world,' Lauren said, 'only lovemaking would be a special thing. It would be the intimate thing, and discussing ideas would be a natural thing.'

'That's a good way to cheapen the exchange of ideas!' someone muttered.

Everyone was laughing and nudging the ones next to them, but my mind was spinning. I bet other kids were about to go out of their minds, too.

Mr Porter ran back and kissed Lauren.

She couldn't seem to stop.

She said, 'What's wrong with a free exchange of ideas?'

'Ideas are personal,' someone said. 'Bodies are all alike, but ideas are individual and personal.'

Mr Porter held Lauren's hand. 'Keep it to yourself, Lauren,' he said. 'Just keep it to yourself.'

'In my opinion,' Lauren began, but Mr Porter had to get her under control, so he just pressed his mouth against hers until she was quiet.

'Don't tell *everything* you're thinking, darling,' he warned her. 'I know this is a class on thoughts, but we have to have *some* modesty.'

Lauren just can't quit. She's a brain, and that mind of hers is going to wander all over the place. It just is. She's that kind of girl.

Sometimes I think I'm that kind of boy, and not the nice boy I claim to be. Do you know what I mean? I want to tell someone what I think about the books I read, not just recite the plots. And I want to ask someone what she thinks about World War II, not just go over its history. And I want to . . .

Never mind.

Listen – the heck with it!

It's not what's up there that counts.

Love makes the world go round. Lovemaking is what's important – relaxing your body, letting your mind empty – just feeling without thinking – just giving in and letting go.

There'll be time enough to exchange ideas, make points – all of it. I'll meet the right girl someday and we'll have the rest of our lives to confide in each other.

'Class come to order!' Mr Porter finally got Lauren quieted down. 'Now, a dream is a succession of images or ideas present in the mind mainly during sleep. It is an involuntary vision . . .'

On and on, while we all reached for each other's hands, gave each other kisses, and got back to normal.

I put that memory out of my poor messed-up mind, and put out my cigarette.

I was ready to face another day, and I told myself, Hey, you're going to be okay. Tonight, you'll get Dad's car, get a date with someone like Edna O'Leary, go off someplace and whisper loving things into her ear, and feel her soft long blond hair tickle your face, tell her you love her, tell her she's beautiful . . .

I swung through the door of the Boys' room, and headed down the hall, whistling, walking fast.

Then I saw Lauren, headed right toward me.

She looked carefully at me, and I looked carefully at her.

She frowned a little. I frowned a lot.

I did everything to keep from blurting out, 'Lauren, what do you think about outer space travel?' . . . 'Lauren, what do you think of Kurt Vonnegut's writing?' . . . 'Lauren, do you think the old Beatles' music is profound or shallow?'

For a moment my mind went blank while we stood without smiling or touching.

Then she kissed my lips, and I slid my arm around her waist.

'Hi, John, dear!' she grinned.

'Hi, Lauren, sweetheart!' I grinned back.

I almost said, 'Would you like to go out tonight?' But it isn't fair to ask a girl out when all you really want is one thing.

I held her very close to me and gently told her that her hair smelled like the sun, and her lips tasted as sweet as red summer apples. Yet all the while I was thinking, Oh, Lauren, we're making a mistake with China, in my opinion . . . Oh, Lauren, Lauren, from your point of view, how do things look in the Middle East?

The Happiest Day of Your Life

Bob Shaw

Jean Bannion held her youngest son close to her, and blinked to ease the sudden stinging in her eyes.

The eight-year-old nestled submissively into her shoulder. His forehead felt dry and cool, and his hair was filled with the smell of fresh air, reminding her of washing newly brought in from an outdoor line. She felt her lips begin to tremble.

'Look at her,' Doug Bannion said incredulously. 'Beginning to sniff! What'd she be like if Philip were going to be away at school for years?' Looming over her as she knelt with the boy in her arms, he patted his wife on the head, looking professional and amused. The two older boys smiled appreciatively.

'Mother is an emotional spendthrift,' said ten-year-old Boyd.

'She has a tendency towards spiritual self-immolation,' said eleven-year-old Theodore.

Jean glared at them helplessly, and they looked back at her with wise eyes full of the quality she had come to hate most since they had travelled the Royal Road – their damnable, twinkling kindness.

'Boys!' Doug Bannion spoke sharply. 'Show more respect for your mother.'

'Thanks,' Jean said without gratitude. She understood that Doug had not reprimanded his sons out of regard for her feelings, but to correct any incipient flaws which might mar their developing characters. Her arms tightened around Philip, and he began to move uneasily, reminding her that she might have been losing him in a few years anyway.

'Philip,' she whispered desperately into his cold-rimmed ear, 'what did you see at the movie we went to yesterday?'

'Pinocchio.'

'Wasn't it fun?'

'*Jean*!' Doug Bannion separated them almost roughly. 'Come on, Philip – we can't have you being late on your one and only day at school.'

He took Philip's hand and they walked away across the gleaming, slightly resilient floor of the Royal Road's ice-green reception hall. Jean watched them go hand-in-hand to mingle with the groups of children and parents converging on the induction suite. Philip's toes were trailing slightly in the way she knew so well, and she sensed – with a sudden pang of concern – that he was afraid of what lay ahead, but he did not look back at her.

'Well, there he goes,' ten-year-old Boyd said proudly. 'I hope Dad brings him into the practice tomorrow – I could do with his help.'

'There's more room in my office,' said eleven-year-old Theodore. 'Besides, the new Fiduciary Obligations Act gets its final reading next week, and I'm going to be involved in a dozen compensation suits. So I need him more than you do.'

They both were junior partners in Doug Bannion's law firm. Jean Bannion looked for a moment into the calm, wise faces of her children and felt afraid. She turned and walked blindly away from them, trying to prevent her features from contorting into a baby-mask of tears. All around her were groups of other parents – complacent, coolly triumphant – and the sight of them caused her control to slip even further.

Finally, she seized the only avenue of escape available. She ran into the Royal Road's almost deserted exhibition hall, where the academy's proud history was told in glowing three-dimensional projections and bland, mechanical whispers.

The first display consisted of two groups of words; pale green letters shimmering in the air against a background of midnight blue. As the slideway carried her past them in silence, Jean read:

> Learning by study must be won;
> 'Twas ne'er entailed from sire to son.
>
> *Gay*

> If only Gay could see us now.
>
> *Martinelli*

The next display unit showed a solid portrait of Edward Martinelli, founder of the academy and head of the scientific research team which had perfected the cortical manipulation complex. A recording of Martinelli's own voice, made a few months before his death, began to drone in Jean's ear with the shocking intimacy of accurately beamed sound.

'Ever since knowledge became the principal weapon in Man's armoury, his chief ally in his battle for survival, men have sought ways to accelerate the learning process. By the middle of the Twentieth Century, the complexity of the human condition had reached the point at which members of the professional classes were required to spend a full third of their useful lives in the unproductive data-absorption phase and . . .'

Jean's attention wandered from the carefully modulated words – she had heard the recording twice before and its emotionless technicalities would never have any meaning for her. The complementary means the academy employed – multi-level hypnosis, psycho-neuro drugs, electron modification of the protein pathways in the brain, multiple recordings – were unimportant to her compared with the end result.

And the result was that any child, provided he had the required level of intelligence, could have all the formal knowledge – which would have been gained in some ten years of conventional high school and university – implanted in his mind in a little over just two hours.

To be eligible, the child had to have an IQ of not less than 140 and a family which could afford to pay, in one lump sum, an amount roughly equal to what the ten years of traditional education would have cost. This was why the faces of the parents in the reception hall had been taut with pride. This was why even Doug Bannion – who made a profession of being phlegmatic – had been looking about him with the hard, bright eyes of one who has found fulfilment.

He had fathered three flawless sons, each with an intelligence quotient in the genius class, and had successfully steered them through the selection procedures which barred the Royal Road to so many. Few men had achieved as much; few women had had the honour of sharing such an achievement . . .

But why, Jean wondered, did it have to happen to me? To *my* children? Or why couldn't I have had a mind like Doug's? So that the Royal Road would bring the boys closer to me, instead of . . .

As the sidewalk carried her on its silent rounds, the animated displays whispered persuasively of the Royal Road's superiority to the old, prolonged, criminally wasteful system of education. They told her of young Philip's fantastic good luck in being born at the precise moment of time in which, supported on a pinnacle of human technology, he could earn an honours law degree in two brief hours.

But, locked up tight in her prison of despair, Jean heard nothing.

Immediately the graduation ceremony was over, Jean excused herself from Doug and the two older boys. Before they could protest, she hurried out of the auditorium and went back to the car. The sun-baked plastic of the rear seat felt uncomfortably hot through the thin material of her dress.

She lit a cigarette and sat staring across the arrayed, shimmering curvatures of the other cars until Doug and the three boys arrived. Doug slid into the driver's seat and the boys got in beside him, laughing and struggling. Sitting in the back, Jean felt shut off from her family. She was unable to take her gaze away from Philip's neat, burnished head. There was no outward sign of the changes that had been wrought in his brain – he looked like any other normal, healthy eight-year-old boy . . .

'Philip!' She blurted his name instinctively.

'What is it, Mother?' He turned his head and, hearing the

emotion in her voice, Theodore and Boyd looked around as well. Three pink, almost-identical faces regarded her with calm curiosity.

'Nothing. I . . .' Jean's throat closed painfully, choking off the words.

'Jean!' Doug Bannion's voice was harsh with exasperation as he hunched over the steering wheel. His knuckles glowed through the skin, the colour of old ivory.

'It's all right, Dad,' ten-year-old Boyd said. 'For most women, the severing of the psychological umbilical cord is a decidedly traumatic experience.'

'Don't worry, Mother,' Philip said. He patted Jean on the shoulder in an oddly adult gesture.

She brushed his hand away while the tears began to spill hotly down her cheeks, and this time there was no stopping them, for she knew – without looking at him – that the eyes of her eight-year-old son would be wise, and kind, and old.

An Ordinary Woman

Bette Greene

I dial the number that for more than twenty years has been committed to memory and then begin counting the rings. One . . . two . . . three . . . four . . . five . . . six – Christ! What's wrong with –

'Newton North High School, good morning.'

'Jeannette? Oh, good morning. This is Armanda Brooks. Look, I may be a few minutes late today. Something came up – no, dear, I'm fine, thanks for asking. It's just a . . . a family matter that I must take care of. I shouldn't be more than ten to twenty minutes late for my first class, and I was wondering if you'd kindly ask one of my students, Dani Nikas, to start reading to the class from where we left off in *The Chocolate War* . . . Oh, that would help a lot . . . Thanks, Jeannette, thanks a lot.'

Aimlessly I wander from bookcase to armchair to table and finally to the large French window that looks out upon my street. Like yesterday and so many yesterdays before, my neighbour's panelled station wagon is parked in the exact spot halfway up their blue asphalt driveway. And today, like yesterday, Roderick Street continues to be shaded by a combination of mature oaks and young Japanese maples.

How can everything look the same when nothing really feels the same? Good Lord, Mandy Brooks, how old are you going to have to be before you finally get it into your head that the world takes no interest in your losses?

The grandfather clock in the hall begins chiming out the

hour of seven and suddenly fear gnaws at my stomach. What am I afraid of now? For one thing, all those minutes. At least thirty of them that I'll have to face alone, here, with just my thoughts.

Calm down now! Its only thirty minutes. Why, the last thing the locksmith said last night was that he'd be here first thing this morning. 'Between seven thirty and eight for sure!'

Anyway, nobody can make me think when I still have the kitchen counter to wipe and breakfast dishes to put into the dishwasher. Thinking hasn't come this hard since Steve's death on the eve of our eighteenth anniversary. That was major league pain all right, but so dear God is this. So is this . . .

No time for that now – no time! Tidying up the kitchen is the only thing that I want to think about. But upon entering the kitchen, I see that with the exception of a mug still half full of undrunk coffee, there is really nothing to do. I pour the now cold coffee into the sink before examining the mug with all those miniature red hearts revolving around the single word MOM.

It was a gift from Caren and not all that long ago either. Maybe a year, but certainly no more than a year ago. But even then I had had suspicions that something wasn't right. Maybe without Caren's loving gift coming at me out of the blue, I would have followed my instincts and checked things out. But frankly I doubt that. The thing is that I wanted – needed – to believe in my daughter.

And going through her drawers in search of I-knew-not-what offended me. It goes against my sense that everybody, even a seventeen-year-old, deserves privacy.

You make me sick, Mandy Brooks, you really do! Just when did you get to be such a defender of the constitutional rights of minors? Why don't you at least have the courage to come on out and tell the truth. Say that, at all costs, you had to protect yourself from the truth. The terrible truth that your daughter, your lovely daughter is a junkie!

Stop it! Stop it! I'm not listening to you anymore. And there's nothing you can do to make me! Steve . . . Steve, oh my God, Steve, how I need you! There hasn't been a day, or even an hour, in all these twenty-two months since you left Caren and me that I haven't needed you. Don't believe those people who observe me from safe distances before patting my wrists and commenting on how strong I am. 'How wonderfully you're carrying on alone.'

Maybe I walk pretty much the same and talk pretty much the same, but, Steve, I don't feel the same. The moment I saw them close the coffin over you, Steve, I knew then what I know now. That the part of me that was most alive and loving got buried down there with you.

So you see, Steve, you've just got to find some way to help us because despite what people say, I'm not strong and I honestly don't know what to do. I look, but I can't find answers, only questions. More and more questions demanding answers: Where did I go wrong with our daughter? Was I too strict? Or too lenient? Did I love her too little . . . or did I love her too much?

Outside a truck door slams. I look at my watch. Five minutes after seven. Could he be here already? I rush to the window to see a white panel truck with black lettering **Newton Centre Locksmiths** at my kerb. And a young man, not all that much older than my seniors, is walking briskly up the front walk.

As he takes the front steps, two at a time, I already have the door open. 'I really appreciate your being so prompt. You're even earlier than you said you'd be.'

'It wasn't me you spoke to. It was my Dad, but when he said that a Mrs Brooks had to have her locks changed first thing in the morning so she wouldn't be late for school, well, I just knew it had to be you.'

'Good Lord, I remember you!' I say, grabbing his hand. 'You were a student of mine!'

He nods and smiles as he holds tightly to my hand. 'You were my favourite English teacher.' Then his eyes drop as though he is taking in the intricate pattern of the hall rug. 'I guess you were my all-time favourite teacher!'

'Oh, that's lovely of you to say, David – your name is David?'

He grins as though I have given him a present. 'David, yes. David Robinson. Hey, you know that's something! You must have had a few hundred students since me. I graduated Newton North two years ago . . . How do you remember all of your students?'

I hear myself laughing. Laughter, it feels strange, but nice. Very nice. 'You give me too much credit, you really do. I'm afraid I can't remember all my students. There have been so many in twenty years. But I think I can probably remember all the students that I really liked.'

He takes in the compliment silently as I ask, 'Your Dad said it wouldn't take long putting in a new cylinder?'

'Ten minutes, Mrs Brooks. Fifteen at the outside . . . How many sets of keys will you need?'

'Sets of keys?' I feel my composure begin to dissolve. Suddenly I'm not sure I can trust my voice, so like an early grade-school child, I hold out a finger. Only one finger.

As I quickly turn to start up the stairs, the acrid smell of yesterday's fire once again strikes my nostrils. Never mind that now! This isn't the time for thinking about what could have been.

But even as I command myself to go non-stop into my bedroom for purse and chequebook and then quickly back down the stairs again, I see myself disobeying.

So I stand there at the threshold of Caren's room staring at the two things that had been burned by fire. Her canopy bed rests on only three legs and where the fourth leg once was there is a basketball-size burn in the thick lime-coloured rug. Her stereo, records, wall-to-wall posters of rock stars, like everything else in this room, are layered with soot.

I remember now that one of the firemen remarked last night that it was sure a lucky thing that the fire had been contained before it reached the mattress. 'You just don't know,' he said, 'how lucky you are.'

How lucky I am? Am I lucky? That's what they used to call me back when I was a high school cheerleader. It all started when Big Joe Famori looked up from the huddle and didn't see me on the sidelines so he bellowed out, 'Where's lucky Mandy?'

But if I really was lucky twenty-five years ago for Big Joe and the Malden Eagles, then why can't I be just a little lucky for the ones I've really loved? 'Cause with a little luck, Steve's tumour could just as easily have been benign, but it wasn't. And with a little luck, Caren could have got her highs from life instead of from drugs. But she didn't.

Luck. Dumb, unpredictable luck. Maybe there's no such

thing as luck. Or maybe I used up all my precious supply on Big Joe Famori and the Malden Eagles. Is that where I failed you, Caren? Not having any more luck to give you?

When you were a little thing, I knew exactly how to make your tears go away. A fresh diaper, a bottle of warm milk, or maybe a song or two while you slept in my arms. That was all the magic I owned, but in your eyes, all power rested in my hands. For you, my love, I lit the stars at night and every morning called forth the eastern sun.

Probably very early on, I should have warned you that your mother was a very ordinary woman with not a single extraordinary power to her name. But, honey, I don't think you would have believed me because I think you needed me to be a miracle mom every bit as much as I needed to be one.

The trouble, though, didn't start until you grew larger and your needs, too, grew in size. And the all-protecting arms that I once held out to you couldn't even begin to cover these new and larger dimensions. Because it wasn't wet diapers or empty stomachs that needed attending to. It was, instead, pride that was shaken and dreams that somehow got mislaid.

So I see now that what from the very beginning I was dedicated to doing, became, of course, impossible to do. And maybe, just maybe, somewhere in the most submerged recesses of our brains, way down there where light or reason rarely penetrates, neither of us could forgive my impotence.

'Mrs Brooks,' David calls from downstairs. 'You're all set now.'

'I'll be right down.' And then without moving from the spot at the threshold, I speak softly to the empty room. Or, more to the point, to the girl who once lived and laughed and dreamed within these walls. 'Caren, dear Caren, I don't know if you're in the next block or the next state. I don't know if I'll see you by nightfall or if I'll see you ever.

'But if you someday return to slip your key into a lock that it no longer fits, I hope you'll understand. Understand, at least, that I'm not barring you, but only what you have become.

'You should know too that if I actually possessed just a

little of that magic that you once believed in, I wouldn't have a moment's trouble deciding how to spend it. I'd hold you to me until your crying stops and your need for drugs fades away.'

David Robinson stands at the bottom of the hall stairs, waiting for me. 'You know, you're a lucky lady, Mrs Brooks,' he says, dropping a single brass key into my hand. 'You're not even going to be late for class.'

Although the centre hall has always been the darkest room in the house, I fumble through my purse for my sunglasses before answering. 'Yes, David,' I say, peering at him through smoke-grey glasses. 'People have always said that about me.'

Well, Well, Well

Kate Hall

'Well you obviously can't keep it.'

'What do you mean, CAN'T keep it? Who says I can't?'

'It's obvious – you'll have to have an abortion.'

'I don't want an abortion. I want to . . .'

'You can't, just think about it for a minute.'

'I have thought about it, I've thought about it a lot.'

'But you've just started college.'

'I know I've started college but there's a crèche there.'

'Oh, I see, you're going to go in pregnant and have the baby in between lectures.'

'It's due in the holidays and anyway I can get time off, other people have done it before, you know.'

'That doesn't mean you have to, though, does it? And what about money?'

'I'll manage.'

'What, on a grant, with a baby and no father?'

'Yes on a grant, with a baby and no father – that's what's really worrying you, isn't it? Bloody hell, in this day and age!'

'Well it would help if you would say who the father is, or don't you know?'

'Of course I know, but I don't want him to.'

'Why not for Christ's sake, he ought to pay for it – you could get maintenance you know or he could pay for an abortion.'

'I don't want him to pay for anything and I am NOT having an abortion.'

'He's not married is he?'

'No, he's not married.'

'Then I don't see . . .'

'I just don't want anyone interfering, that's all.'

'Well you needn't worry on my account – I'm not having anything to do with it and don't expect me to baby-sit either.'

'No one asked you to.'

'Not yet, but just you wait. Honestly, I thought YOU were old enough to know better. It's embarrassing.'

'You'll be saying "What will the neighbours say?" next.'

'I don't give a damn about the neighbours but they will think things if there's no father.'

'There is a father!'

'Oh yes, an anonymous one.'

'I KNOW who he is.'

'Well at least tell me.'

'No. Look, I made a decision, I got pregnant on purpose. I want to have this baby, okay?'

'BUT MUM – at your age!'

The Toy Girl

Paula Clark

The grass was wet against her face and smeared her as she looked up. Irregular shifting shapes surrounded her in the darkness and laughter grew from one side and shimmered over her head. One of the shapes reached out and touched her shoulder – 'Paula?'

The voice, incredibly loud, ricocheted inside her head. She winced and squinted to focus on the blank face, dissolving into helpless, wheezy giggles when the shape became Helen, her eyes wide and amazed.

Arms lifted her (or pulled her down) and half carried her, mumbling and weak, across the damp park. She could hear voices swirling through the vapour in her mind, some familiar, some not, some from outside, some from within. 'Drunk? She's *blasted*! What was she *doing*?'

Her kitchen appeared from somewhere and she was sat down, blinking in the hard electric light. She looked absently at her hands. They were bruised with the cold but she felt nothing and the uncomprehending giggling bubbled uncontrollably out of her.

The house seemed full of people. Their voices and movements blurred around her and vaguely she heard the cupboard doors open and hungry hands reach inside and take. The words asking them not to formed in her mind but diffused into confused sobbing and mumbling before they reached her mouth. She could hear pop music from somewhere and a muffled fear turned in her stomach, but then the light began to dim around the edges and the sound to spin away and darkness flowed over the room.

The wrenching inside her own head woke her up. Aware of a throbbing silence and, strangely, the heavy smell of paint in the room, she ached her eyes open and blinked painfully around her. The image which faced her made her recoil in horror, taking a sudden, frightened breath. The walls . . . oh my *God* the walls . . . paint . . . Random sprayed lines dribbled across them, coating the ripped wallpaper as it hung like jagged leaves around her. The pounding in her head grew and her stomach tumbled as she saw the room completely now, smashed and littered, a red wine stain seeping like blood in the corner of the carpet. She sat up, spinning, trembling, her mouth horribly dry as fear burned in her throat. She walked almost dreamlike through the house as though it were some weird, undiscovered cave. It was totally unfamiliar, a sickening mixture of garish, hateful colour and destruction.

What had they *done*? She stared disbelievingly around her, a cold numbness spreading inside her and beginning to squeeze hot tears down her face. The sweet, gluish smell of vomit grew in the hallway and as she heard the crunch of her parents' car in the drive she stood, uncertain, caught between the two. As the key scraped in the lock, the discarded Toy Girl wiped her eyes and, reaching down, gently picked up a torn piece of paper from the floor. She curled herself up in the corner by the stairs and pressed her face into her knees, her trembling hands tightly clutching the tiny fragment of a birthday card.

Slipper Satin

Alex La Guma

4

The street couldn't have changed much in four months. The same two rows of houses were there, with their fenced stoops and verandas; the same Indian grocery shop, and the back of the warehouse that had a big sign painted across the whole expanse of wall. There were the same grey pavements, cracked in places. Perhaps the paint and colour-wash on the houses had faded and peeled somewhat during the four months, and there were wide streaks down the wall of the warehouse, damaging the big black lettering.

And the people were there, too. The little knots of twos and threes at the gates of some of the houses, the row of idle men against the warehouse wall, and the children playing in the gutters. Nothing had really changed in the street.

She stared straight ahead as she came into the street, but sensed the wave of interest that stirred the people. Recognition tapped them on the shoulder, and she felt the faces turning toward her. There was a little flurry among the group at one gate, or at a fence, and then it ran on quickly and mysteriously to the next, and the next, down the street, so that the women peered slyly at first, murmuring among themselves, watching her approach, and then breaking into loud chatter when she had passed.

'That is she . . . that's she . . .'

'Got four months, mos', for immorality . . .'

'Come home again, hey? We don't want damn whores on this street.'

And the needle-sharp eyes followed her all the way, suspicious, angry, and secretly happy, too, that there was another victim for the altars of their gossiping.

With the men it was different. They watched her come, some openly, some from under the rims of their lowered eyelids, watching her and smiling gently at the thought of her conquest. Who the hell cared if it had been a white boy? He had been lucky enough, hadn't he? A man didn't begrudge another that kind of victory, even if it had been across the line. A man was a man, and a girl a girl. She was still around, anyway, so maybe there was a chance for one of them.

They were amused at the stupid malice of the womenfolk, and they showed their defiance by saying, 'Hullo, Myra. How you, Myra? Nice to see you again, Myra. How you keeping, Myra?' And they felt the stares of the women, too, and grinned at the girl to show that it was okay with them.

She smiled gently, hearing their voices, but kept her head up and her eyes forward. But she felt the bitterness inside her like a new part of her being. She had finished with crying, and crying had left the bitterness behind like the layer of salt found in a pan after the water had evaporated. So that even as she smiled there was a scornful twist to her mouth.

She was tall and brown and good-looking, with the fullness of lips, the width of cheekbone, the straight nose and firm chin, and the blue eyes that she had inherited from the intermarriage of her ancestors generations past. Her body was firm, a little hardened from hard work for four months, but still beautiful; the breasts full and wide at the bases, the belly flat and the thighs and legs long and shapely.

She reached the house at last and climbed the steps onto the veranda. When she opened the front door the smell of cooking came to her from the kitchen at the end of the passageway. The old smell of frying onions and oil.

She walked down the passage and there was the elderly woman, her mother, standing over the pots on the black iron stove, short and stout, with thinning hair tied in a knot at the back of her head.

Myra leaned against the jamb of the kitchen door, a small panic struggling suddenly inside her. But she fought it off and said, casually, 'Hullo, Ma.'

Her mother looked around with a jerk, a big stirring spoon,

poised over a saucepan, in the thick, scrubbed hand that shook a little. Myra looked into the decaying, middle-aged eyes and saw the surprise replaced slowly by hardness, the twist of the elderly mouth, the deep lines in the throat and neck, and the network of wrinkles.

'Oh. So you're back. Back with your shame and disgrace, hey?'

'I'm back, Ma,' Myra said.

'You brought disgrace on us,' her mother said harshly, the spoon waving in the girl's face. 'We all good and decent people, but you brought us shame.' The face crumbled suddenly and tears seeped out of the eyes. 'You brought us shame. You couldn't go and pick a boy of your own kind, but you had to go sleep with some white loafer. You brought us shame, after how I worked and slaved to bring you up. Nobody ever been to jail in our family, and you a girl, too. It's enough to give an old woman a stroke, that's what it is.'

Myra gazed at her mother and pity edged its way forward at the sight of a work-heavy body, the ruined face, the tears, but something else thrust pity aside and she said steadily, 'It wasn't any disgrace, Ma. It's no disgrace to love a man, no matter what colour he is or where he comes from. He was nice and he wasn't what you call a white loafer. He would have married me if he could. He always said so.'

'What's the matter with your own kind of people? What's the matter with a nice coloured boy?' The quavering voice sobbed and hiccoughed and the girl felt a pang of revulsion.

'There's nothing wrong with coloured boys,' she said, more in irritation than anger. 'Nobody said there was anything wrong with coloured boys. I happened to fall for a white boy, that's all.'

'It's no better than being a whore,' the old woman sobbed. 'No better than that.'

'All right,' the girl said bitterly. 'I'm no better than a whore. All right. Leave it like that. I'm a whore and I brought you disgrace. Now then.'

'Don't you talk to your own Ma like that!' The old woman began to shout angrily, waving the spoon about. 'You got a cheek to talk to your poor Ma like that, after all I done for you. You haven't got respek, that's what. Got no respek for your betters. There's your sister Adie getting married soon. To a nice boy of her own kind. Not like you. Getting married and a fine example you are for her. You. You. Yes, you.'

'I'm glad Adie's getting married,' Myra said with forced dryness. 'I hope to God her husband takes her away to go and live on their own.'

'You haven't got no respek, talking to your mother that way. Just shows what kind you are. Adie at least been supporting me while you been in that disgrace, in that jail for four months. And now you just come to bring bad luck into the house. You bad luck, that's what you are.'

Myra smiled a little scornfully and said, 'All right, I'm a whore and a disgrace and bad luck. All right, Ma. But don't worry. You won't starve with me around.'

'If you get a job,' the mother snapped. 'And if I was a boss I wouldn't give no damn whore a job.'

'Oh, stop it, Ma. You'll make yourself sick.'

'Ja. And whose fault will that be?'

Myra looked at the hysterical old woman for a second and then turned away. She felt like crying, but she was determined not to. She'd had enough of crying. She left the old woman and turned into the room off the passageway.

It was still the same room, with the wardrobe against one wall and the dressing table between the two single beds where she and her sister Ada slept. She lay down on her bed in her clothes and stared at the ceiling.

Ada getting married. She was genuinely glad about that. She and Ada had always been very close. She thought, no Mixed Marriages Act and no Immorality Act and maybe I'd be getting married, too, but you got four months in jail instead of a wedding. Poor old Tommy.

She began to wonder whether Tommy really had been serious about loving her. No, he must have been. He really had been. He had loved her, but it must have proved too much for him. But what did he have to go and do that for? If he had loved her that bad he would have stuck it out, no matter what. Maybe Tommy just couldn't see any other way. So that night when the police had come in on them he'd gone from the bedroom into the living room and to his desk, and before they knew anything about it he had the little automatic pistol out of the drawer and had shot himself.

So that was that. Poor Tommy. Maybe he thought it was a

disgrace, too. Maybe he thought that, in spite of all his love. But she didn't care any more.

She lay on the bed and tried not to think about it. She thought about Ada instead. She would like to give Ada a nice wedding present. She wouldn't go to the wedding ceremony, of course. She'd save the dear old family the embarrassment. But she'd have to give Ada a nice wedding present.

And then in the middle of her thoughts the front door banged, feet hurried along the passageway, and the door opened and there was Ada.

'Myra. Myra, ou pal. You're back.'

Her younger sister was there, flinging bag and jacket aside, and hugging her. 'I heard those damn old hens up the street cackling about my sister, and I just ran all the way.'

'Hullo, Adie. Good to see you again. Give me a kiss. Yes, I think they'll be cackling a long time still.' She added bitterly, 'The old woman feels the same.'

'Don't you worry, bokkie. Hell, I'm glad you're back for the wedding.'

'How's the boy friend?'

'Okay.' Ada grinned at her sister. 'He doesn't give a damn. His family had things to say, of course. But I've got him like that.' She showed a fist, laughing. 'He'll listen to Adie, family or no family.'

'You got everything ready?'

'Oh, yes. The wedding dress will be ready the end of the week, on time for Saturday. I managed to save and bought some stuff for the house. Joe put in for one of those Council cottages and they said we can move in.'

'I'll miss you.'

'Garn. You can mos' come and visit us any time. Listen, if you like I could talk to Joe about you coming to stay with us. What do you say?'

'No. You go off on your own and be happy. I'll stay on here. Me and Ma will maybe fight all the time, but I'll manage.'

'What you going to do, Myra?'

'Don't know,' Myra told her. 'The old lady will need looking after. Say, have you really got everything?'

'Oh, yes. Except maybe the frock to change into next Saturday night. I'll have to wear the wedding dress right through the whole business. I did see the damn nicest party frock at the Paris Fashions, but I suppose I'll have to do without a change on Saturday night. It's so lousy having to wear the wedding dress at the party, too. Things and stuff might spill onto it. The bride ought to change for the evening celebrations. We're having a party at Joe's place. I thought it'd be grand to have a dress to change into, though. But I worked out every penny, so I won't be able to afford eight guineas. Such nice darn slipper satin, too. Real smart.'

Ada got up from the edge of the bed and started removing her work clothes. 'Tell me, Myra, was it bad up there?'

'Not too bad. I did washing most of the time. But I don't want to talk about it, man.'

'We won't,' Ada smiled, struggling into black stovepipe jeans. 'That's all finished and done with. Now you just take it easy and I'll call you when supper's ready. You like some tea?'

'Thanks.'

Ada grinned and ducked out of the room, leaving Myra alone again on the single bedstead. Dear old Ada, with a whore for a sister. The old woman would probably say it would be bad luck to have me coming visiting them. She felt sorry for her mother, for Ada, for all those women up the street, for Tommy. Poor old Tommy. Tommy couldn't stand up to it. Him and his love. Him and his I love you. She had died, too, she thought, the instant Tommy pulled the trigger. Poor old Tommy. She felt sorry for all of them.

She thought, Adie is going to be happy. She wanted Adie to be happy and she told herself that Adie would have that slipper satin dress she wanted, as a present from her. She could earn eight guineas easily.

The Dead Woman

Sarah Baylis

Nurse Moonie's on duty again, pissed off at being put on this boring ward that isn't maternity, isn't intensive care, but somehow a ghoulish mixture of the two. *Bloody liberty. They just want someone who'll keep her mouth shut.*

Nurse Moonie always keeps her mouth shut. She's all eyes, no mouth, hoovering up impressions and keeping information stuffed inside her like a hamster: she has dirt on everyone now – everyone except her patient, of course, who is unabatingly good and endlessly silent. *Mum*, snorts Nurse Moonie, *is the word.*

Her patient is a dead woman. Snow White, laid out pale as a lily in a casket of crystal – as pretty as Snow White – and as uncomplaining. Instead of seven dwarfs scurrying about this winking casket, polishing the chrome, seven nurses and seven doctors.

It wasn't an apple that carried her off, but a mighty haemorrhage which pounded the delicate folds of her brain to a pulp and drowned them in a tide of crimson. Nothing could be seen from outside except the delicate fainting of a woman to the floor, and this was followed by grief, the howl of sirens and a screech of ambulance tyres as the woman's husband dealt efficiently with the demise of his wife.

Now she lies beneath a bank of sterile equipment. At her head gleams a quarter of a million pounds' worth of chips and tubes and quartz; at her feet another half million's worth of humming generator and something that looks like the hub cap of a car. She cannot breathe, so scentless oxygen is squeezed into her flaccid lungs. She cannot eat, so liquid pap is squirted into her veins. She doesn't shit; she leaks. No word, she utters, no sigh. Her cheek is as pale as milk and her lips are shut tight, like folded paper. Her blood, pushed through her body by a whirring pump, is as thin and lustreless as gruel.

But, ahh, purrs Nurse Moonie, *she has a man to love her.*

The dead woman's husband is a caring fellow. His gentle face is often seen by the casket side as he sits by his wife's bed and holds her icy hand, sometimes even uttering a phrase or two in her deaf ear. He loves her. She is completely dead, but she has something even now that makes his heart beat fast enough for two, that makes his pulse race and his forehead bead with sweat. *Poor sap,* scoffs the Nurse, *it'll bring him nothing but sorrow.*

She shuddered and fetched her duster. In this sterile place where did the dust come from? Did it flake off the dead woman's very face in a last attempt at jinxing the machinery? Did the air produce it? Was there some contagion in the woman's lungs that puffed it out at every exhalation, like pneuma? Certainly everyone got depressed on this ward. It was a gloomy place, this plastic sepulchre; the gloom settled everywhere, as silently as dust. The only thing that makes death bearable is that it hurries in and hurries out, whisking away the soul and leaving a little staleness in the air that can be cured by throwing wide the windows and waving a feather duster at the corners of the room. Here in this squeaky ward, death hung about, lingering; was tied down, even, by the bank of bleeping dials that sent the gruel sloshing relentlessly through dead collapsing veins.

Nurse Moonie lifted her skirt and scratched her knee. Flea bites from the cat. She sniggered at the thought of bringing a few of the little creatures in with her. Would they feed off dead flesh as eagerly as they fed off her? She shrugged and stared out of the window, feeling ill. It was her job to move the cold, shrivelling arms and wash the armpits where hair still grew; to readjust the catheters. It was horrible, this tending of a corpse, unnatural; a laying-out that went on for months. *What am I, after all,* she asked herself, *a bloody undertaker*? She was starting to hate her own sex, so closely did she have to observe each colourless pucker of her patient. She was becoming squeamish, and that's bad news for a nurse.

Midday, and here come the doctors. Squeak, squeak, and a whiff of aftershave; hands behind backs and as solemn as churchmen.

Up for a knighthood, Dr Stone is as excited as the day he first got a place in the school cricket team. He rubs his hands and peers at his own personal mausoleum – woman-shaped: how novel!

'Nurse Moonie? How do we progress?'

'We progress marvellously, doctor, thank you.'

Nurse Moonie stands behind the dead woman and speaks for her, feeling strangely protective. Pretty golden hair floats on the pillow. The dead woman's flesh is more vulnerable than ever, pearly blue and easily marred, as Dr Stone hoists up the rough gown and displays the dead nakedness to all and sundry. Behind him, the young doctors shift and sway and peer through spectacles.

'Behold, gentlemen, our very own little miracle,' and the prospective knight fishes for an old-fashioned ear trumpet and presses it to the dead woman's large abdomen. His old doctor's mouth curved in a smile. What does he hear, save the ordinary gurgles of this artificially sustained life?

'Our baby's doing nicely,' he beams, and looks just like a chef sniffing out a pot of sauce.

Polite applause from the young doctors, and Nurse Moonie sneers privately. She hates this fleshy coffin of a woman, and yet she could kill these grinning consultants for their pursuit of creation. She would stand in front of the glass casket and flail about her with a scalpel to save this dead woman from these final indignities. What good can come of it, after all, bringing a child into the world from a dead woman's belly? What succour for an infant with only a dead breast to suck? *Ugh, poor little fool, motherless even before your time. Nurtured in a bloody grave! What'll it be doing to your soul, growing in such a silent, unfeeling place?*

Yet Nurse Moonie knows that this baby born of a dead mother will rest in her arms as sweet and slippery as any other. She has her superstitions (and she hates the doctors for their heartless procreation) but she is a warm-hearted woman and will sniff the baby's head and speak to it in the high, trance-like voice that babies love; she will weep seeing it raw and alone in its incubator like a hatched chick; and she will cry angrily when the dead woman's husband comes to claim his seed.

Off duty, now, Nurse Moonie. Here comes the night sister, whisking along, full of news. Time to go home.

Once out of the pure, clear air of the ward, Nurse Moonie is tossed into the echoing corridors of the hospital, a warren of groaning Victorian inconvenience. Here the living shuffle about and balls of real homely dust scuttle along the lino. Like a modern witch, Nurse Moonie is anxious to be home with her cat, a vicious creature of elegance and haphazard temper. She's eager to wash the smell of death off her hands. Being a living woman, Nurse Moonie is menstruating, and she wants to put her feet up and close her eyes, and forget about the dead womb of her patient that has no choice but to keep carrying its charge.

When she opens the door, the cat yowls and she gives it milk.

The Watcher

J. California Cooper

I have always, always tried to do right and help people. It's a part of my community duty and my duty to God. But I can tell you right now, you don't never get no thanks for it! For nothin you do! My life ain't been no bed of roses either, but I still takes my time to do for others. Not one person has thanked me!

I ain't feared of nothin but God and white folks! God, cause He is the boss! White folks, cause they runs this world and they don't know what they doing! Don't talk sense! You ever hear them shows on television where they talkin bout Law and Order? They use up all them big words in them long sentences and ain't said nothin but somethin to help themselves! Seems they dance all around the least thing to answer everything and then the show be over and they ain't settled nothin! I try to holler and tell em but they don't want to listen to nobody! But I do, I *do* try to help other people as my religious duty.

Use to be a big ole fat sloppy woman live cross the street went to my church. She had a different man in her house with her every month! She got mad at me for tellin the minister on her bout all them men! Now, I'm doin my duty and she got mad! I told her somebody had to be the pillar of the community and if it had to be me, so be it! She said I was the pill of the community and a lotta other things, but I told the minister that too and pretty soon she was movin away. Good! I like a clean community!

Take that woman over there up the corner, cross the

street. Now, she got five kids with that husband she got and she thought they was happy just cause they was well-fed and all, but there's more to life than that! Now I knew her husband was foolin round with that Dorothy woman on the side. Her house joins theirs from the backyard, but on another street. I went over there tryin to help her by tellin her all about it, but she got mad at *me* and told me to get out of her house! Well, I left cause I know it's some people you can't do a good turn for. She not only put me out, she put *him* out! I don't know where he went, but I do know what I was talkin bout cause I seen him with my own eyes!

See, some nights I go up there to a place where people park in the dark. I be lookin to see is my daughter up there or is she wherever she sposed to be. I seen this car just a bouncing round in the night. It looked like that man's car so I said maybe he was sick in there or something and maybe I better do my duty as a human being and help him! But when I shined my flashlight in the window, I didn't see nothin but booty flying, chile! He wasn't sick! He had plenty strength to look up and cuss me all kinds of names! Me, a religious woman! Trying to help him! Anyway, I left there and came straight home to ease my heart and first chance I got I did my duty and tole his wife! He done made all them babies at home and he out there in the car tryin to make some more! Honey, I don't know about some people! But that ain't all! After she put him out, she had the nerve to come to my house and ask me for some money for food for them kids of hers! They ain't mine! I told her I didn't have nothin to give nobody and she better put the police on that busy behind of her husband's! She didn't speak to me no more, but I did my duty and I don't care! Wasn't too long fore they got back together and they moved. One thing I can say bout this street, people always moving. I been here longer than anybody!

Now, there was a man and a nice woman use to live on the side of me. He was a really heavy drinker tho. He didn't never fight his wife, but he threaten to sometimes. He brought his pay home and all, all of it, his wife said. I don't know where he got money for that liquor from, but he did. I liked his wife and felt sorry for her so I called her mama and told her what her daughter was going through, then I called his mama and told her what kind of son she had. She was a fool cause she hung up on me. Then I called Alcohol Anonymous and told them to come over to his house, like I was his wife, cause I know she never would have the grit to do it. Then I called the police and told them to watch out for his drivin and gave them the licence number, all that, for his good and her good! Well, one night right after that, she was cryin when he really had done hit her (I knew he would one day!) for callin' all them calls! So I told her that he should not beat her cause it was really me tryin to help her! She jumped up and you see this scratch right here cross my whole face, don't you? Well, she put it there! Just for me tryin to help her! They done moved away now. Good!

Oh, I have my troubles tryin to help people! My cross to burden! Just at that time my daughter had to go to the hospital! Seem she had tried to abortion herself, right there in her room, and she was so quiet I didn't notice nothin about it and she was bout to die when her daddy noticed and took her on to the hospital. That was on the night I usually go to check that dark parkin spot for her, so she was already in the hospital when I came home . . . and had to rush over there! A good person's work is never done, I tell you! When she was better, I ask her when she got that baby, how did it happen? She say, in her own room! Her own room! When I be out doin my errands of mercy and also tryin to protect her, that's what she do to me! Now, my son didn't give me that kind of trouble. He just stay in his room or go out for a little visit sometime. He go to high school and work part-time, a good young man. When he wasn't readin, he be sleepin when he is home. No trouble at all!

Now about that time, too, the couple what lived over on the other side of me, the woman had just got herself a job downtown there in a insurance agency. They was always kinda doing poorly with money. But when I seen she was gettin some new clothes and going out of that house every day looking prettier and better, I knew something was wrong somewhere! She was getting another man! Don't you see? Well, I changed my insurance over to the company she was working for and I commence to go down there to see about it, and I would see her sometimes with a pencil and a pad in her hand. Well, that pencil and pad didn't fool me!

I'm too smart for that! She would go in a room with a man and close the door! Close the door! Honey, you can't fool me.

Well, I was out in my garden one day after that, did a lot of work in my garden that week, and finally her husband came out with the garbage and I told him he better protect himself cause of what was happenin in his own house under his own nose. Well, I thought he had some sense! I heard them arguing that night and I heard the gunshot too! He had done shot her! I prayed for her tho and so she didn't die. But she moved on away when she came out the hospital. I could have told that man that she was gonna leave him when she got that job! Anyway, she left. Now, I didn't mean for all that to happen, bullets and everything! Sometimes you can't help people, cause they ain't got sense enough to know what to do! And I shouldn't have helped him anyway, cause he don't know right! That was his baby my daughter was gettin rid of, I found out!

That's another thing, bout that time my daughter ran off with one of them card-playing double-dealin suckers that hang around the Buzzards Nest nightclub. She gone now. I don't know where. After all the protection I tried to give her! I still go on my midnight trips to the parkin place, done got in a habit of lookin after my chile! But one thing I can't get over is my daughter tellin me fore she left, I didn't pay her no mind . . . no attention, that she couldn't talk to me! Now one thing I do know . . . I was a good mother to that child! Telling me that! But God don't like ugly and one day she be back, needin me!

Now, the worsest thing was the woman what lived right directly cross the street from me. She was a nice enough lookin woman, but she wasn't married and she always dressed real nice and she worked. I never did see no company coming over there cept her mama or somebody like that, but I knew something had to be going on wrong! A single woman!? Lookin that good and all!? Don't you see? Well, ain't nobody else on this block gonna do it and somebody has to care about the community and all, so I took to watching over there all day and didn't never see nothin so I took to stayin up watchin that house all night! I wished I was two people so I could watch at the back of her house too! I'm a very steady person, my mama used to always tell me that, so I was steady on my job. My husband used to call me to come to bed. I told him no, I had a job to do. I knew what he wanted anyway!

Well, six months passed and still I ain't seen nothin! I figured it must be happening when I had to get some sleep, so I made my husband watch when he was home and I slept. He didn't like it at first but he soon understood what I meant, least I thought so. Do you know what happened? They made friends! In a month, they was talkin! Then everything was interrupted! My son died! From an overdose of heroin, the doctor and the police say. Right back there in that room! In my house! He was so quiet, sleep or readin! A mother can't see everything. And we had no sooner buried him, my husband and me, when my husband left me and filed for his divorce! Now HE the one I see going in that woman's house across the street! And he told me they was gonna get married! And move. He kept sayin they was gonna move! Lord, lord, lord, what must I bear?! I been a good wife and a good mother, all my time was given to the betterment of my family and see here what I done got! Ain't no thanks in this world!

Well, I just got a job to do, that's all! To hold up my community! When a lady, bout my age, moved in next door to me where that man had moved from, I told her about this world and this community and told her she could help me clean out the bad ones. But she said, 'Leave it to God to judge.' See that? Her religion don't mean nothin to her! Leave it to God! I am one of his deciples! I have the miraculous gift! I do His work! She told me I was a fool! And I was wrong!! Well, after I jumped on her and beat her up, yes I did! Yes I did! You don't talk to no deciple like that! Anyway, after I beat her behind, she told my minister, the same one I used to talk to. That man had nerve to open his mouth and tell me she was right and I was wrong! I knew he was the devil then! I almost quit goin to his church but I changed my mind. I don't sit up in the front no more tho, I sit way in the back. I ain't through! I'm watching her, that lady next door. I'm watching that minister too! There is a sin there somewhere! I don't take much time to sleep now, ain't nobody here but me, noway.

I stay here . . . in this window, on my job . . . Watching!

Fatal Woman

Joyce Carol Oates

♃

The first, the very first time, I became aware of my power over men, I was only twelve years old.

I remember distinctly. Because that was the year of the terrible fire downtown, the old Tate Hotel, where eleven people were burned to death and there was such scandal. The hotel owner was charged with negligence and there was a trial and a lot of excitement. Anyway, I was walking downtown with one of my girl friends, Holly Turnbull, and there was a boardwalk or something by the hotel, which was just a ruin, what was left of it, and you could smell the smoke, such an ugly smell, and I was looking at the burnt building and I said to Holly: 'My God do you smell *that*?' Thinking it was burnt flesh. I swear it was. But Holly pulled my arm and said 'Peggy, there's somebody watching us!'

Well, this man was maybe my father's age. He was just standing there a few yards away, watching me. He wore a dark suit, a white shirt, but no tie. His face was wrinkled on one side, he was squinting at me so hard his left eye was almost closed. You'd think he was going to smile or say something funny, grimacing like that. But no. He just stared. Stared and stared and stared. His lips moved but I couldn't hear what he said – it was just a mumble. It wasn't meant for me to hear.

My hair came to my waist. It was light brown, always shiny and well-brushed. I had nice skin: no blemishes. Big brown eyes. A pretty mouth. Figure just starting to be what it is today. I didn't know it, but that man was the first, the very first, to look at me in that special way.

He scared me, though. He smelled like something black and scorched and ugly. Holly and I both ran away giggling, and didn't look back.

As I grew older my attractiveness to men increased and sometimes I almost wished I was an elderly woman! – free at last from the eyes and the winks and the whistles and the remarks and sometimes even the nudges. But that won't be for a while, so I suppose I must live with it. Sometimes I want to laugh, it seems so silly. It seems so crazy. I study myself in the mirror from all angles and I'm not being modest when I say that, in my opinion, I don't *seem* that much prettier than many women I know. Yet I've been in the presence of these women and it always happens if a man or a boy comes along he just skims over the others and when he notices me he stares. There must be something about me, an aura of some kind, that I don't know about.

Only a man would know.

I got so exasperated once, I asked: What is it? Why are you bothering *me*? But it came out more or less humorously.

Gerry Swanson was the first man who really dedicated himself to me – didn't just ogle me or whistle or make fresh remarks – but really fell in love and followed me around and ignored his friends' teasing. He walked by our house and stood across the street, waiting, just for a glimpse of me, and he kept meeting me by accident downtown or outside the high school, no matter if I was with my girl friends and they all giggled like crazy at the sight of him. Poor Gerry Swanson, everybody laughed. I blushed so, I couldn't help it. It made me happy that he was in love with me, but it frightened me too, because he was out of school in a few years and seemed a lot older than the boys I knew. (I had a number of boy friends in high school – I didn't want to limit myself to just one. I was very popular; it interfered with my schoolwork to some extent, but I didn't care. For instance, I was the lead in the Spring Play when I was only a sophomore, and I was on the cheerleading squad for three years, and I was First Maid-in-Waiting to the Senior Queen. I wasn't voted Senior Queen because, as my boy friends said, all the girls were jealous of me and deliberately voted against me, but *all* the boys voted for me. I didn't exactly believe them. I think some of the girls probably voted for me – I had lots of friends – and naturally some of the boys would have voted for other candidates. That's only realistic.) When Gerry came along, I was sixteen. He was working for his father's construction company and I was surprised he would like a girl still in high school, but he did; he telephoned all the time and took me out, on Sundays mainly, to the matinée downtown, because my father didn't trust him, and he tried to buy me things, and wrote letters, and made such a fool of himself everybody laughed at him, and I couldn't help laughing myself. I asked him once what it was: *Why* did he love me so much?

He just swallowed and stared at me and couldn't say a word.

As I've grown older this attractiveness has gradually increased, and in recent weeks it has become something of a nuisance. Maybe I dress provocatively – I don't know. Certainly I don't amble about with my bare midriff showing and legs bare up to the buttocks, like many other girls, and I've recently had my hair cut quite short, for the warm weather. I have noticed, though, that my navy-blue dress seems to attract mention; possibly it fits my body too tightly. I don't know. I wish certain men would just ignore me. For instance, a black man on the street the other day – a black *police*man, who should know better – was staring at me from behind his sunglasses with the boldest look you could imagine. It was shocking. It was really rude. I gave him a cold look and kept right on walking, but I was trembling inside. Later, I wondered if maybe I should have pretended not to notice. I wondered if he might think I had snubbed him because of the colour of his skin – but that had nothing to do with it, not a thing! I'm not prejudiced in any way and never have been.

At the hospital there are young attendants, college-age boys, at the very time of life when they are most susceptible to visual stimulation; they can't help noticing me, and staring and staring. When I took the elevator on Monday to the tenth floor, where Harold's room is, one of the attendants hurried to get on with me. The elevator was empty except for us two. The boy blushed so his face went beet-red. I tried to make things casual by remarking on the weather and the pretty petunias out front by the sidewalk, but the boy was too nervous and he didn't say a word until the door opened on the tenth floor and I stepped out. 'You're so beautiful!' – he said. But I just stepped out and pretended not to hear and walked down the corridor.

Eddie telephoned the other evening, Wednesday. He asked about Harold and I told him everything I knew, but then he didn't say goodbye, he just kept chattering and chattering – then he asked suddenly if he could come over to see me. That very night. His voice quavered and I was just so shocked! – but I should have seen it coming over the years. I should have seen it coming. I told him it was too late, I was going to bed, but could he please put my daughter on the phone for a minute? That seemed to subdue him.

In church I have noticed our minister watching me, sometimes out of the corner of his eye, as he gives his sermon. He is a few years younger than I am, and really should know better. But I've had this certain effect all my life – when I'm sitting in an audience and there are men addressing the group. I first noticed it, of course, in junior and senior high school, but it didn't seem to be so powerful then. Maybe I wasn't so attractive then. It's always the same: the man addressing us looks around the room, smiling, talking more or less to everyone, and then his eye happens to touch upon me and his expression changes abruptly and sometimes he even loses the thread of what he is saying, and stammers, and has to repeat himself. After that he keeps staring helplessly at me and addresses his words only to me, as if the rest of the audience didn't exist. It's the strangest thing . . . If I take pity on him I can somehow 'release' him, and allow him to look away and talk to the others; it's hard to explain how I do this – I give a nearly imperceptible nod and a little smile and I *will* him to be released, and it works, and the poor man is free.

I take pity on men, most of the time.

Sometimes I've been a little daring, I admit it. A little flirtatious. Once at Mirror Lake there were some young Italian men on the beach, and Harold saw them looking at me, and heard one of them whistle, and there was an unpleasant scene . . . Harold said I encouraged them by the way I walked. I don't know: I just don't know. It seems a woman's body sometimes might be flirtatious by itself, without the woman herself exactly knowing.

The telephone rang tonight and when I picked up the receiver no one answered.

'Eddie,' I said, 'is this Eddie? I know it's you, dear, and you shouldn't do this – you know better – what if Barbara finds out, or one of the children? My daughter would be heart-broken to know her own husband is making telephone calls like this – You know better, dear!'

He didn't say a word, but he didn't hang up. I was the one to break the connection.

When I turned off the lights downstairs just now, and checked the windows, and checked the doors to make sure they were locked, I peeked out from behind the living-room shade and I could see someone standing across the street, on the sidewalk. It was that black policeman! But he wasn't in his uniform. I don't think he was in his uniform. He's out there right now, standing there, waiting, watching this house. Just like Gerry Swanson used to.

I'm starting to get frightened.

Everyone tells me to be strong, not to break down – about Harold, they mean; about the way the operation turned out. Isn't it a pity? they say. But he's had a full life, a rich life. You've been married how long – ? Happily married. Of course. And your children, and the grandchildren. 'A full, rich life.' And they look at me with that stupid pity, never seeing me, not *me*, never understanding anything. What do I have to do with an old man, I want to scream at them. What do I have to do with an old dying man?

One of them stood on the sidewalk that day, staring at me. No, it was on a boardwalk. The air stank with something heavy and queer and dark. I giggled, I ran away and never looked back. Now one of them is outside the house at this very moment. He's waiting, watching for me. If I move the blind, he will see me. If I snap on the light and raise the blind even a few inches, he will see me. What has he to do with that old man in the hospital, what have I to do with that old man . . .? But I can't help being frightened.

For the first time in my life I wonder – what is going to happen?

Uncle Ifor's Welsh Dresser

Pat Lacey

12 The Close,
London SW.
30th January

Brewsham & Moore,
Estate Agents,
Farnfield.

Dear Sir,

Would you please send me particulars of any three bed-roomed houses for sale in the Farnfield area which are in a good state of repair, adjacent to the local primary school, near open countryside and have a good garden. Most important of all, they must have a very large kitchen.

I do hope you can help me.

Yours faithfully,
Jennifer Clarke

Brewsham & Moore,
Farnfield.
3rd February

Ms J Clarke,
12 The Close,
London SW.

Dear Ms. Clarke,

Thank you for your letter. I enclose particulars of several properties, but would point out that it was impossible to comply with all your requirements. As you will see, 'Ashling', in Meadow

Lane, complies with most of them; there is a primary school at the end of the lane for the children, there are open fields, at the other end of the lane, the garden is a reasonable size, although somewhat overgrown, and the kitchen, although you do not give exact specifications, is large ('Ashling' was once a farmhouse).

However, the house has been allowed to fall into a certain state of disrepair – its previous owner was an elderly lady who is now living with her daughter – although nothing, I would have thought, would be beyond the capabilities of a reasonably competent D.I.Y. enthusiast to manage alone.

If you wish to inspect the property, I will be available to show you around all week.

Yours sincerely,
David Moore

12 The Close.
4th February

Dear Mr. Moore,

Thank you for your letter and enclosures.

My elderly aunt and I will arrive at Farnfield station at 10.45 this Saturday. Unless I hear that you would prefer not to have him in your car, I should like to bring Meredith, my Border Collie. He is not very big, loves trains and sulks if left at home by himself; the last time, he ate the rubber plant and was very ill. The rubber plant was not improved, either. Normally, I would have brought my own car, but it has to go in for servicing.

By the way, perhaps I should explain the reasons for my very precise requirements; the primary school is for me, as I am a teacher; the garden is for Aunt Hetty who has wanted one ever since she gave up her own to come and look after me in our flat when my parents died; the open fields are for Meredith; the kitchen is for Aunt Hetty's Welsh dresser (Uncle Ifor, who died many years ago, made it for her when they were first married and she refuses to part with it), and the good state of repair is for my fiancé Mark, who could not, I'm afraid, be described as a 'reasonably competent D.I.Y. enthusiast'. However, he is a *very* competent executive with a large oil company and is actually in the Middle East at the moment for a month. Meanwhile, I am fairly competent with a hammer and chisel, and Aunt Hetty is not above holding the nails.

I hope you will forgive these autobiographical details, but I thought it might help if you were aware of the situation.

Please don't hesitate to say if you would prefer not to have Meredith. I can always leave the rubber plant with friends!

Yours sincerely,
Jennifer Clarke

Brewsham & Moore.
6th February

Dear Miss Clarke,

I shall be at Farnfield station at 10.45 on Saturday, the 8th, and look forward to meeting you.

Please bring Meredith – and the measurements of Aunt Hetty's Welsh dresser.

Yours sincerely,
David Moore

12 The Close.
10th February

Dear David,

Thank you for being so kind to us on Saturday. I had no idea that estate agents could be so helpful. I must apologise again about the hole Meredith made in your car seat. I think he was over-excited after the journey. You *must* let me pay for it.

Both Aunt Hetty and I loved Ashling. And I am sure Mark would, too. If only the kitchen was two inches longer! However, Aunt Hetty still seems to think we can get her dresser in and suggests that she re-takes the measurements and we try again this Saturday. Perhaps I could collect the key from the office this time, to save you the bother? I shall have my car back tomorrow.

Yours sincerely,
Jenny.

Lyndhurst,
The Rise, Farnfield.
10th February

Dear Jenny,

I feel I must write and set your mind at rest about the slight tear Meredith made in my car seat cover. It's nothing that a patch won't take care of!

I'm so glad you like Ashling. As I explained, the old lady to whom it belongs is my grandmother; she is in no hurry to sell as long as it goes to someone who'll love it as much as she does.

I can quite understand why your Aunt Hetty wants to keep your uncle's Welsh dresser. Clearly, it was a labour of love. If only he had made it two inches shorter! However, I don't think the problem is insurmountable. My grandmother tells me that the inside kitchen wall was put up about twenty years ago in order to make the breakfast room, and could easily be removed without harming the original structure. Perhaps you and Aunt Hetty would like to come down again and see what I mean. What about this Saturday?

Yours sincerely,
David

12 The Close.
16th February

Dear David,

Thank you for yesterday. Meredith and I both adored our walk. I think early spring is always the best time for woods, don't you? Mind you, in a few months' time I shall be saying the same thing about the summer! I do hope I shall be able to see the daffodils that you say grow down by the stream. Oh, why didn't Uncle Ifor make Aunt Hetty a nice little coffee table or a set of dining-room chairs!

However, even though we've now found out that it's too high as well as too long, Aunt Hetty is still hopeful! She wants to come down yet again to see if we can take the floor tiles up or cut a hole in the ceiling! Could you bear it? I must say, she and your grandmother seemed to have got on very well. Now she knows there are gentians in the rockery, she's more determined than ever to live at Ashling.

Meredith sends his love and says he's not really afraid of rabbits. But being a town dog, he'd just never seen one before!

Yours,
Jenny

P.S. Mark will be home in a fortnight. Perhaps he will have a bright idea about the dresser.

Lyndhurst,
Farnfield.
16th February

Dear Jenny,

That was a splendid walk we had yesterday! I haven't been in Bramble Woods for years – not since Gran used to get us to go blackberrying for her. I'm sorry Meredith was frightened by that rather ferocious rabbit.

It's a shame about Uncle Ifor's dresser. I suppose we couldn't saw a bit off the bottom? Ask Aunt Hetty what she thinks and then come down and we'll measure once more.

If you could manage Saturday again, there's an old James Stewart film on at the local cinema club. I remember you saying how much you liked him. Mum says she and Gran would love to look after Aunt Hetty and Meredith.

Yours,
David

Lyndhurst,
Farnfield.
23rd February

Dear Jenny,

I hope you enjoyed the film. Too bad Aunt Hetty forgot to bring the new measurements. What about next Saturday? I promise I won't try to kiss you again. I don't know what came over me. At least, that's not strictly true – you looked so pretty in that fluffy thing you were wearing, I just didn't think twice. I certainly forgot you were an engaged woman. Please forgive me! I'll make sure it doesn't happen again.

Yours,
David

12 The Close,
London SW.
27th February

Brewsham & Moore,
Estate Agents,
Farnfield.

Dear Mr. Moore,

I am writing to make an appointment for my fiancé Mark Johnson to view Ashling, Meadow Lane. I trust that 10.30 a.m. next Wednesday would be convenient? If I do not hear to the contrary, I will arrange for him to meet you at the house.

Yours sincerely,
Jennifer Clarke

12 The Close,
London SW.
6th March

Brewsham & Moore.

Dear Sir,

Ashling, Meadow Lane, Farnfield

Please note that I am no longer interested in the purchase of this property.

Yours faithfully,
J. Clarke

12 The Close.
6th March

David,

I am sending this to your home address because there are one or two things I must say that would not be suitable for your secretary to read. To begin with, there was absolutely no need for you to point out to Mark all the things that needed doing at Ashling – and then try to sell him a newer house. You'd never even mentioned to me that the roof leaked!

And there was no necessity for you to be so pessimistic about Uncle Ifor's dresser! I'm sure we could have found a way, somehow. Not that we'll have the chance now, as

Mark and I are no longer speaking to each other, and our engagement is off. As I couldn't possibly manage the mortgage repayments on my own, the purchase of Ashling is off, too. Aunt Hetty has taken to her room and refuses to talk about it.

I never thought you could be so underhand and deceitful. I can only imagine that your feelings clouded your professional judgment.

Jenny

P.S. There is no point in coming to see us. Anyway, I won't be here – I am going to stay with friends in Norfolk.

Lyndhurst.
8th March

Dear Jenny,

I hope that Aunt Hetty will send this letter on to you.

I was very sorry indeed that you felt you must break off negotiations for Ashling. And I can assure you that I had nothing at all to do with Mark's reaction. I didn't even go with him to view it, but sent our junior partner Stephen Watson, instead.

I must admit that my feelings for you over the last few weeks have grown far beyond the limits of a business relationship, but your happiness will always come first. Under the circumstances, I quite understand why you do not wish to continue with the purchase of Ashling, but I hope very much that we will not lose touch.

David

Norfolk.
13th March

Dear David,

Aunt Hetty sent on your letter. I'm sorry I'd got it all wrong. It never occurred to me that someone else would show Mark around Ashling and he wouldn't know you from Adam.

I'm still very mixed up about everything. Aunt Hetty says it's bound to take time. Thank you for everything.

Jenny

Lyndhurst.
8th September

Dear Jenny,

I thought you might like to know that Ashling has now been sold, but that the new owner has had it converted into two separate flats, one of which is available for rent. Would you and Aunt Hetty be interested? I'm sure Meredith would! Please come and see for yourselves. How about Saturday?

Yours,
David

P.S. You missed the daffodils but the blackberries are early this year in Bramble Woods.

12 The Close.
14th September

Darling David,

It was wonderful to see you again. And the blackberries are out of this world. As you say, the ground floor would be best for Aunt Hetty.

You didn't have to be so devious! I would have come to see it, even if I had known you would be our landlord! See you next Saturday. Come for the day, if possible, and I'll book a theatre.

Love,
Jenny

P.S. Strange – but Aunt Hetty hasn't even mentioned the dresser!

Lyndhurst.
19th September

Dearest Jenny,

I think you know how happy I am that you and Aunt Hetty will be coming to live at Ashling. See you on Saturday.

All my love,
David

P.S. I didn't dare mention the dresser – d'you think Aunt Hetty has forgotten about it?

Lyndhurst.
22nd September

My dear Aunt Hetty,

Jenny has passed on your congratulations on our engagement. Thank you! You know how pleased I am that you will be occupying the ground floor flat while Jenny and I have the top.

It is most *kind to want to give us Uncle Ifor's dresser for a wedding present but I really don't think we would get it up that narrow staircase.*

Your affectionate
nephew-to-be,
David

12 The Close.
24th September

Dear David,

No one has ever given my Ifor credit for being the excellent craftsman that he was!

The whole thing will take apart and bits can be left out or added, to make it narrower, shorter, taller, without altering its basic design.

I never told either you or Jenny this because it made a good excuse for continuing to visit Ashling while you got to know each other better (I never did think Mark a suitable match for her). Certainly, there would be no problem in getting it up your stairs! However, it has served its purpose and I've decided to spare you. Much better if you and Jenny buy the furniture you really want.

So I shall have it downstairs in my kitchen, and send you a cheque instead.

Your devious but loving,
Aunt Hetty.

Stench of Kerosene

Amrita Pritam

Outside, a mare neighed. Guleri recognised the neighing and ran out of the house. The mare was from her parents' village. She put her head against its neck as if it were the door to her father's house.

Guleri's parents lived in Chamba. A few miles from her husband's village which was on high ground, the road curved and descended steeply downhill. From this point one could see Chamba lying a long way away at one's feet. Whenever Guleri was homesick she would take her husband, Manak, and go up to this point. She would see the homes of Chamba twinkling in the sunlight and would come back, her heart glowing with pride.

Once every year, after the harvest had been gathered in, Guleri was allowed to spend a few days with her parents. They sent a man to Lakarmandi to bring her back to Chamba. Two of her friends, who were also married to boys who lived away from Chamba, came home at the same time and the girls looked forward to their annual reunion, talking about their joys and sorrow. They went about the streets together. Then there was the harvest festival when the girls would have new clothes made for the occasion. Their *dupattas* would be dyed, starched and sprinkled with mica to make them glisten. They would buy glass bangles and silver ear-rings.

Guleri always counted the days to the harvest. When autumn breezes cleared the skies of monsoon clouds, she thought of little else. She went about her daily chores – fed the cattle, cooked food for her parents-in-law – and then sat back to work out how long it would be before someone came to fetch her from her parents' village.

And now, once again, it was time for her annual visit. She caressed the mare joyfully, greeted her father's servant, Natu, and made preparations to leave the next day. She did not have to express her excitement in words: the look on her face was enough. Her husband pulled at his *hookah* and closed his eyes. It seemed as if he either did not like the tobacco or that he could not bear to face his wife.

'You'll come to the fair at Chamba, won't you? Come even for a day,' she pleaded.

Manak put aside his *chillum* but did not reply. 'Why don't you answer me?' she asked, a little cross. 'Shall I tell you something?'

'I know what you're going to say – that you only go to your parents once a year. Well you've never been stopped before.'

'Then why do you want to stop me this time?' she demanded.

'Just this once,' he pleaded.

'Your mother's said nothing so why do you stand in the way?' Guleri was childishly stubborn.

'My mother . . .' Manak did not finish his sentence.

On the long-awaited morning, Guleri was ready long before dawn. She had no children and therefore no problem of having to leave them behind or take them with her. Natu saddled the mare as she took leave of Manak's parents. They patted her head and blessed her.

'I'll come with you for part of the way,' Manak said.

Guleri was happy as they set out. She hid Manak's flute under her *dupatta*.

After the village of Khajiar, the road descended steeply to Chamba. There she took out the flute and gave it to him. She took his hand in hers and said, 'Come now, play your flute.' But Manak, lost in his thoughts, paid no heed. 'Why don't you play your flute?' she asked, coaxing him. He looked at her sadly. Then putting the flute to his lips, blew a strange anguished wail.

'Guleri, don't go away,' he begged her. 'I ask again, don't go away this time.' He handed the flute to her, unable to continue.

'But why?' she asked. 'Come over on the day of the fair and we'll return together, I promise you.'

Manak did not ask again.

They stopped by the roadside. Natu took the mare a few paces ahead to leave the couple alone. It crossed Manak's mind that it was at this time of the year, seven years ago, that he and his friends had come on this very road to go to the harvest festival in Chamba. And it was at this fair that Manak had first seen Guleri and they had bartered their hearts to each other. Later, managing to meet her alone, he remembered taking her hand and telling her, 'You are like unripe corn – full of milk.'

'Cattle go for unripe corn,' Guleri had replied, freeing her hand with a jerk. 'Human beings prefer it roasted. If you want me, go and ask my father for my hand.'

Among Manak's kinsmen it was customary to settle the bride price before the wedding. Manak was nervous because he did not know the price Guleri's father would demand from him. But Guleri's father was prosperous and had lived in cities. He had sworn that he would not take money for his daughter but would give her to a worthy young man from a good family. Manak, he decided, answered these requirements and soon after, Guleri and Manak were married. Deep in memories, Manak was roused by Guleri's hand on his shoulder.

'What are you dreaming of?' she teased him.

He did not answer. The mare neighed impatiently and Guleri got up to leave. 'Do you know the bluebell wood a couple of miles from here?' she asked. 'It's said that anyone who goes through it becomes deaf. You must have passed through that bluebell wood. You don't seem to be hearing anything I say.'

'You're right, Guleri. I can't hear anything you're saying to me,' and Manak sighed.

They looked at each other. Neither understood the other's thoughts. 'I'll go now,' Guleri said gently. 'You'd better go back. You've come a long way from home.'

'You've walked all the distance. You'd better get on the mare,' replied Manak.

'Here, take your flute.'

'You take it.'

'Will you come and play it on the day of the fair?' she asked with a smile. The sun shone in her eyes. Manak turned his face away. Perplexed, Guleri shrugged her shoulders and took the road to Chamba. Manak returned home.

He entered the house and slumped listlessly on the *charpoy*. 'You've been away a long time,' exclaimed his mother. 'Did you go all the way to Chamba?'

'Not all the way, only to the top of the hill.' Manak's voice was heavy.

'Why do you croak like an old woman?' said his mother severely. 'Be a man.'

Manak wanted to retort, 'You are a woman; why don't you cry like one for a change!' But he remained silent.

Manak and Guleri had been married seven years but she had never borne a child and Manak's mother had made a secret resolve that she would not let it go beyond the eighth year. This year, true to her decision, she had paid five hundred *rupees* to get him a second wife and she was waiting, as Manak knew, for Guleri to go to her parents before bringing in the new bride. Obedient to his mother and to custom, Manak's body responded to the new woman but his heart was dead within him.

In the early hours one morning he was smoking his *chillum* when an old friend happened to pass by. 'Ho, Bhavani, where are you going so early in the morning?'

Bhavani stopped. He had a small bundle on his shoulder. 'Nowhere in particular,' he said evasively.

'You should be on your way to some place or the other,' exclaimed Manak. 'What about a smoke?'

Bhavani sat down on his haunches and took the *chillum* from Manak's hands. 'I'm going to Chamba for the fair,' he said at last.

Bhavani's words pierced through Manak's heart like a needle.

'Is the fair today?'

'It's the same day, every year,' replied Bhavani drily. 'Don't you remember, we were in the same party seven years ago?' Bhavani did not say any more but Manak was conscious of the other man's rebuke and he felt uneasy. Bhavani put down the *chillum* and picked up his bundle. His flute was sticking out of the bundle. Manak's eye remained on the flute till Bhavani disappeared from view.

Next morning, Manak was in his fields when he saw Bhavani coming back but he looked the other way deliberately. He did not want to talk to Bhavani to hear anything about the fair. But Bhavani came round the other side and sat down in front of Manak. His face was sad and grey as a cinder.

'Guleri is dead,' Bhavani said in a flat voice.

'What?'

'When she heard of your second marriage, she soaked her clothes in kerosene and set fire to them.'

Manak, mute with pain, could only stare and feel his own life burning out.

The days went by. Manak resumed his work in the fields and ate his meals when they were given to him. But he was like a dead man, his face blank, his eyes empty.

'I am not his wife,' complained his second wife. 'I'm just someone he happened to marry.'

But quite soon she was pregnant and Manak's mother was pleased with her new daughter-in-law. She told Manak about his wife's condition, but he looked as if he did not understand and his eyes were still empty.

His mother encouraged her daughter-in-law to bear with her husband's moods for a few days. As soon as the child was born and placed in his father's lap, she said, Manak would change.

A son was duly born to Manak's wife; and his mother, rejoicing, bathed the boy, dressed him in fine clothes and put him in Manak's lap. Manak stared at the new-born babe in his lap. He stared a long time, uncomprehending, his face as usual expressionless. Then suddenly the blank eyes filled with horror and Manak began to scream. 'Take him away!' he shrieked hysterically, 'Take him away! He stinks of kerosene.'

dupatta a long shawl worn with traditional Indian dress
hookah a pipe consisting of a tube attached to a vessel (for smoking)
chillum a clay pipe (for smoking)
charpoy a type of bed
rupee Indian currency

Another Evening at the Club

Alifa Rifaat
translated by Denys Johnson-Davies

In a state of tension, she awaited the return of her husband. At a loss to predict what would happen between them, she moved herself back and forth in the rocking chair on the wide wooden verandah that ran along the bank and occupied part of the river itself, its supports being fixed in the river bed, while around it grew grasses and reeds. As though to banish her apprehension, she passed her fingers across her hair. The spectres of the eucalyptus trees ranged along the garden fence rocked before her gaze, with white egrets slumbering on their high branches like huge white flowers among the thin leaves.

The crescent moon rose from behind the eastern mountains and the peaks of the gently stirring waves glistened in its feeble rays, intermingled with threads of light leaking from the houses of Manfaicut scattered along the opposite bank. The coloured bulbs fixed to the trees in the garden of the club at the far end of the town stood out against the surrounding darkness. Somewhere over there her husband now sat, most likely engrossed in a game of chess.

It was only a few years ago that she had first laid eyes on him at her father's house, meeting his gaze that weighed up her beauty and priced it before offering the dowry. She had noted his eyes ranging over her as she presented him with the coffee in the Japanese cups that were kept safely locked away in the cupboard for important guests. Her mother had herself laid them out on the silver-plated tray with its elaborately embroidered spread. When the two men had taken their coffee, her father had looked up at her with a smile and had told her to sit down, and she had seated herself on the sofa facing them, drawing the end of her dress over her knees and looking through lowered lids at the man who might choose her as his wife. She had been glad to see that he was tall, well-built and clean-shaven except for a thin greying moustache. In particular she noticed the well-cut coat of English tweed and the silk shirt with gold links. She had felt herself blushing as she saw him returning her gaze. Then the man turned to her father and took out a gold case and offered him a cigarette.

'You really shouldn't, my dear sir,' said her father, patting his chest with his left hand and extracting a cigarette with trembling fingers. Before he could bring out his box of matches, Abboud-Bey had produced his lighter.

'No, after you, my dear sir,' said her father in embarrassment. Mingled with her sense of excitement at this man who gave out such an air of worldly self-confidence was a guilty shame at her father's inadequacy.

After lighting her father's cigarette, Abboud-Bey sat back, crossing his legs, and took out a cigarette for himself. He tapped it against the case before putting it in the corner of his mouth and lighting it; then he blew out circles of smoke that followed each other across the room.

'It's a great honour for us, my son,' said her father, smiling first at Abboud-Bey, then at his daughter, at which Abboud-Bey looked across at her and asked:

'And the beautiful little girl's still at secondary school?'

She had lowered her head modestly and her father had answered:

'And from today she'll be staying at home in readiness for your happy life together, Allah permitting,' and at a glance from her father she had hurried off to join her mother in the kitchen.

'You're a lucky girl,' her mother had told her. 'He's a real find. Any girl would be happy to have him. He's an Inspector of Irrigation, though he's not yet forty. He earns a big salary and gets a fully furnished government house wherever he's posted, which will save us the expense of setting up a house – and I don't have to tell you what our situation is – and that's besides the house he owns in Alexandria where you'll be spending your holidays.'

Samia had wondered to herself how such a splendid suitor had found his way to her door. Who had told him that Mr Mahmoud Barakat, a mere clerk at the Court of Appeal, had a beautiful daughter of good reputation?

The days were then taken up with going the rounds of Cairo's shops and choosing clothes for the new grand life she would be living. This was made possible by her father borrowing on the security of his government pension. Abboud-Bey, on his part, never visited her without bringing a present. For her birthday, just before they were married, he brought her an emerald ring that came in a plush box bearing the name of a well-known jeweller in Kasr el-Nil Street. On her wedding night, as he put a diamond bracelet round her wrist, he had reminded her that she was marrying someone with a brilliant career in front of him and that one of the most important things in life was the opinions of others, particularly one's equals and seniors. Though she was still only a young girl she must try to act with suitable dignity.

'Tell people you're from the well known Barakat family and that your father was a judge,' and he went up to her and gently patted her cheeks in a fatherly, reassuring gesture that he was often to repeat during their times together.

Then, yesterday evening, she had returned from the club somewhat lightheaded from the bottle of beer she had been required to drink on the occasion of someone's birthday. Her husband, noting the state she was in, hurriedly took her back home. She had undressed and put on her nightgown, leaving her jewellery on the dressing table, and was fast asleep seconds after getting into bed. The following morning, fully recovered, she slept late, then rang the bell as usual and had breakfast brought to her. It was only as she was putting her jewellery away in the wooden and mother-of-pearl box that she realised her emerald ring was missing.

Could it have dropped from her finger at the club, in the car on the way back? No, she distinctly remembered it last thing at night, remembered the usual difficulty she had in getting it off her finger. She stripped the bed of its sheets, turned over the mattress, looked inside the pillow cases, crawled on hands and knees under the bed. The tray of breakfast lying on the small bedside table caught her eye and she remembered the young servant coming in that morning with it, remembered the noise of the tray being put down, the curtains being drawn, the tray then being lifted up again and placed on the bedside table. No one but the servant had entered the room. Should she call her and question her?

Eventually, having taken two aspirins, she decided to do nothing and await the return of her husband from work.

Directly he arrived, she told him what had happened and he took her by the arm and seated her down beside him:

'Let's just calm down and go over what happened.'

She repeated, this time with further details, the whole story.

'And you've looked for it?'

'Everywhere. Every possible and impossible place in the bedroom and the bathroom. You see, I remember distinctly taking it off last night.'

He grimaced at the thought of last night, then said:

'Anybody been in the room since Gazia when she brought in the breakfast?'

'Not a soul. I've even told Gazia not to do the room today.'

'And you've not mentioned anything to her?'

'I thought I'd better leave it to you.'

'Fine, go and tell her I want to speak to her. There's no point in your saying anything, but I think it would be as well if you were present when I talk to her.'

Five minutes later Gazia, the young servant girl they had recently employed, entered behind her mistress. Samia took herself to a far corner of the room while Gazia stood in front of Abboud-Bey, her hands folded across her chest, her eyes lowered.

'Yes, sir?'

'Where's the ring?'

'What ring are you talking about, sir?'

'Now don't make out you don't know. The one with the green stone. It would be better for you if you hand it over and then nothing more need be said.'

'May Allah blind me if I've set eyes on it.'

He stood up and gave her a sudden slap on the face. The girl reeled back, put one hand to her cheek, then lowered it again to her chest and made no answer to any of Abboud's questions. Finally he said to her:

'You've got just fifteen seconds to say where you've hidden the ring or else, I swear to you, you're not going to have a good time of it.'

As he lifted up his arm to look at his watch the girl flinched slightly but continued in her silence. When he went to the telephone, Samia raised her head and saw that the girl's cheeks were wet with tears. Abboud-Bey got through to the Superintendent of police and told him briefly what had occurred.

'Of course I haven't got any actual proof but seeing that no one else entered the room, it's obvious she's pinched it. Anyway I'll leave the matter in your capable hands. I know your people have their ways and means.' He gave a short laugh, then listened for a while and said: 'I'm really most grateful to you.' He put down the receiver and turned round to Samia:

'That's it, my dear. There's nothing more to worry about. The Superintendent has promised me we'll certainly get it back. The patrol car's on the way.'

The following day, in the late afternoon, she'd been sitting in front of her dressing table re-arranging her jewellery in its box when an earring slipped from her grasp and fell to the floor. As she bent to pick it up she saw the emerald ring stuck between the leg of the table and the wall. Since that moment she had sat in a state of panic awaiting her husband's return from the club. She even felt tempted to walk down to the water's edge and throw it into the river so as to be rid of the unpleasantness that lay ahead.

At the sound of the screech of tyres rounding the house to the garage, she slipped the ring onto her finger. As he entered she stood up and raised her hand to show him the ring. Quickly, trying to choose her words but knowing that she was expressing herself clumsily, she explained what an extraordinary thing it was that it should have lodged itself between the dressing table and the wall, what an extraordinary coincidence she would have dropped the earring and so seen it, how she'd thought of ringing him at the club to tell him the good news but . . .

She stopped in mid-sentence when she saw his frown and added weakly:

'I'm sorry. I can't think how it could have happened. What do we do now?'

He shrugged his shoulders as though in surprise.

'Are you asking me, my dear lady? Nothing of course.'

'But they've been beating up the girl – you yourself said they'd not let her be till she confessed.'

Unhurriedly, he sat himself down as though to consider this new aspect of the matter. Taking out his case, he tapped a cigarette against it in his accustomed manner, then moistened his lips, put the cigarette in place and lit it. The smoke rings hovered in the still air as he looked at his watch and said:

'In any case she's not got all that long before they let her go. They can't keep her for more than forty-eight hours without getting any evidence or a confession. It won't kill her to put up with things for a while longer. By now the whole town knows the servant stole the ring – or would you like me to tell everyone: "Look, folks, the fact is that the wife got a bit tiddly on a couple of sips of beer and the ring took off on its own and hid itself behind the dressing table? What do you think?"'

'I know the situation's a bit awkward . . .'

'Awkward? It's downright ludicrous. Listen, there's nothing to be done but to give it to me and the next time I go down to Cairo I'll sell it and get something else in its place. We'd be the laughing-stock of the town.'

He stretched out his hand and she found herself taking off the ring and placing it in the outstretched palm. She was careful that their eyes should not meet. For a moment she was on the point of protesting and in fact uttered a few words:

'I'd just like to say we could . . .'

Putting the ring away in his pocket, he bent over her and with both hands patted her on the cheeks. It was a gesture she had long become used to, a gesture that promised her continued security, that told her that this man who was her husband and the father of her child had also taken the place of her father who, as though assured that he had found her a suitable substitute, had followed up her marriage with his own funeral. The gesture told her more eloquently than any words that he was the man, she the woman, he the one who carried the responsibilities, made the decisions; she the one whose role it was to be beautiful, happy, carefree. Now, though, for the first time in their life together, the gesture came like a slap in the face.

Directly he removed his hands her whole body was seized with an uncontrollable trembling. Frightened he would notice, she rose to her feet and walked with deliberate steps towards the large window. She leaned her forehead against the comforting cold surface and closed her eyes tightly for several seconds. When she opened them, she noticed that the cafe lights strung between the trees on the opposite shore had been turned on and that there were men seated under them and a waiter moving among the tables. The dark shape of a boat momentarily blocked out the cafe scene; in the light from the hurricane lamp hanging from its bow she saw it cutting through several of those floating islands of Nile waterlilies that, rootless, are swept along with the current.

Suddenly she became aware of his presence alongside her.

'Why don't you go and change quickly while I take the car out? It's hot and it would be nice to have supper at the club.'

'As you like. Why not?'

By the time she had turned round from the window, she was smiling.

'Til Death Us Do Part

Jacqueline Brine

She lay with her fingers stuck hard in her ears. There was no sound.

Every so often she quickly, for a brief brief second, took the finger out of her left ear. There was a sudden change in the pitch, the tone, of the silence. It was working: good! She knew it worked, anyway, because she had used this method of shutting herself down, every night, for the last few years. But still she had to take one of the fingers out every so often – it was always the left one, her right finger was jammed solid between her right ear and the pillow. The sound of her own silence, in her own head, would reach such intensity that she began to doubt the existence of anything or anyone else. There was only her, her head trapped within itself.

She could never really tell anyone. If asked, she would say to her mother, 'No, I'm not scared; yes, of course I can sleep; no, I didn't hear anything last night'; and sometimes, trying to be funny, she would say, 'Oh, I just stick my fingers in my ears!' But she never told anyone of how she would lie in bed, hot, the sweat pouring off her, her heart beating fast, and she would then go so cold she felt as if she were freezing from within; or of how, encased in her own silence, her imagination would hear noises outside of her window.

She never told how she thought she saw him climbing up the drainpipe to the window, how he reached his left leg over to the window-sill and, balancing himself, tapped gently on the window until the catch was released; how his hand came in, reached down, and opened the large window; how then, holding on to the gaping window frame, he pulled himself across and, pushing the curtains in front of him, he climbed onto her bed. At this point she always pulled both fingers out, forced herself to open her eyes, and listening, looking, with the full force of her senses, she stared, tight within her taut body, into the room.

Her mouth was dry, her breath quick: she listened, her entire body was a huge ear; her stomach thumped, she felt sick; she stifled her screams; she tried to calm herself, to convince herself that she was safe, that it was only her imagination. She wished he were dead, and then, as soon as she wished, she felt guilty, but she knew she meant it. She wanted, more than anything else, to feel free, to be free of Him.

She wanted to go to her mother, to be held by her like she guessed she'd been held when she was a child, but she knew she couldn't. She couldn't tell her mother she was scared; she couldn't tell her that she was almost sick with terror. Her mother thought her strong, capable and sensible. Her mother depended on her. She had to look after her mother, she had to protect her. But she knew she wasn't *that* strong, she knew she was scared, and she longed desperately for someone to see that she was.

She coughed, hoping that a brother, her sister or her mother, would cough back. They never talked about it, but they all took reassurance from these coughs. A cough from one of the other bedrooms meant that there was somebody else in the house who was awake; it meant that she was not so totally alone as she thought.

If there were no answering coughs, she knew, just as certainly, that she was alone. There was her, the night, and the fear. She would lie there, like a statue, feeling the responsibility for the whole family like a dead weight upon her young body.

The silence whistled in her ears, and the sound of her swallowing was magnified out of all proportion. She thought of the axe in the coal cellar, pushed right to the back and hidden by broken, stinking fish boxes and her father's old coats; but he knew it was there too, somewhere, and if he wanted it, he'd get it. He'd smash the kitchen door down and would come into the house, up the stairs, and into their bedrooms, whilst, all the time, they slept.

She tried to think of other things, of nice things, fantasising her own happy future. She would replace her fingers in her ears: the second finger of the right hand and the first finger of the left, fitting perfectly into their respective sockets. The whistle changed down into a deep hum. She was tired and she wanted to sleep, but there was always a part of her wide awake, listening, through her fingers, always listening.

She heard the tapping sound again. It was very close. She listened: nothing. She tried to sleep. Tap, scratch, tap: awake again. Nothing. She didn't have enough strength left to keep her fingers in her ears: the left one slipped out. Tap, scratch, tap, tap: she nearly died of total fright; she nearly cried with relief. For it was nothing more than her own eyelashes brushing against the sheet. Her body heavy, and her fingers plugged into her head, she finally fell into exhausted sleep.

She awoke slowly to find the silvery winter sun shining through the window. Another night gone. She stumbled out of bed and into clothes; she had to go to work. She went down the stairs into the kitchen. Everyone was talking: not arguing as they normally did in the morning: they were talking.

Her mother's eyes were red, her mouth trembling, her hands shaking. Her brothers and sisters started to shout: fast and angry, but with shock, fear and inadequacy; not really knowing how to comfort the woman holding on to the sink for support. They all started to tell her at once, jumbling over their own words and each other's. The middle-aged woman, with her head almost in the sink full of dirty dishes, was crying again; one hand was trying to hold her face together, but between the fingers she could see the flesh disintegrating. She couldn't understand what they were all saying, but she understood that she had to go outside. She stood on the doorstep, her face white. Her thin lips became thinner, pinching themselves into her mouth. There, on the path, between the kitchen door and the open door of the coal cellar, was laid out, in tiny lumps of coal, the word:

JOANIE

She could see the coats and boxes which hid the axe. It was still there. But He'd been there. HE'D been there again last night. He'd left the message. He'd been there, outside, whilst they slept, inside. With painstaking care He'd taken the coals and placed them, one by one, on the path, knowing that each lump of each letter would burn into the flesh of the woman standing by her dirty sink.

She heard her mother's voice. She felt the pressure, the responsibility, the guilt knot the back of her neck. As she turned around she kicked the bits of coal away with a sudden angry movement of her foot. Trying to keep her voice as calm as she could, she replied, 'No Mum, I went straight to sleep; I didn't hear anything.'

The Headache

Ann Hunter

As she lifted the shopping bag off the hall floor it dripped blood. Dull red on the polished parquet, it plopped steadily, so that Joanna stood transfixed, remembering.

'What on earth . . . of course, it must be the liver. How stupid of me . . .'

She rushed across the hall through the dining room, leaving the telltale stains like a paper-chase, and finally heaved the bag into the sink where it could drip without spoiling anything.

'Now where's the floorcloth . . . Mrs Renwick's always rearranging these cupboards . . . I must tell her not to . . . Will blood stain the carpet? What should I use? Cold water first, I think.'

It was soon under control. Wiping the blood off the parquet flooring was easy, but seeing it there, that small puddle, she remembered . . .

Joanna Nicholls prided herself on her beef stroganoff. It was her speciality. When guests came who had already sampled its delights, they begged for a second performance; those who hadn't, wished to be initiated. And so Joanna cooked vast quantities, ladled it into polythene containers and froze it in the 'gynormous' chest freezer in the back of the second garage. James had recently learnt this new word at school, and used it to describe anything bigger than himself.

Tonight the guests were important. Charles needed a loan – a big one – for extensions to the surgery. The bank manager and his wife, plus one of the senior partners and his wife were coming, ostensibly for a splendid stroganoff, in reality for business negotiations. Joanna sighed, pushing back the damp tendrils of hair from her forehead as she tasted the sauce.

'I don't find freezing it makes it stronger; it needs more pepper in it.'

'The table's finished.'

'Oh, thanks. You can pop off now if you want, Mrs Renwick. There's not much else to do. And thanks for doing such a lovely job with the flowers. See you Thursday.'

Mrs Renwick always looked so plump and healthy. The epitome of good nature . . . how could she seem so happy, so relaxed, with that minute house, those awful children, no car, no money . . .

'See you Thursday then. Hope you have a nice evening.'

Nice? No, it'll be the usual hell of putting on a brave face . . . and being bored to tears.

Joanna replaced the heavy pot in the oven and went over to the mirror. She felt she still looked attractive, but there was no doubt that she was a mature woman. The wrinkles – laugh lines Charles called them – round her eyes were very definite now, but her hair was still lovely. Soft curls, brown and silky – always gave her an Edwardian look when she wore her hair up – like tonight. She fussed briefly with the ruffles of her white blouse, arranging the locket so that it lay smoothly on the frothy lace cravat, then walked slowly into the lounge.

Charles sprawled on the sofa reading the *Lancet*. He didn't look up.

If only he'd talk to me now, before they all come. Treat me like a human being and not a piece of furniture . . . or a T.V. only switched on when being looked at.

'Had a busy day?'

'Mm. Yes. Usual. Everything ready?'

'Yes. Fine. Like a drink?'

'No, I've already got one, thanks.'

And me. What about me? Or do I have to get my own?

Joanna went to the drinks cupboard and poured a gin – a big gin with very little tonic. The ice clinked comfortingly in the glass and she inhaled the heady perfume before taking a first tingling sip. All so peaceful. So ordinary. James. I haven't said goodnight to him.

'Have you said goodnight to James?'

'No – give him a kiss for me will you, Jo.'

Again. Always give him a hug – a kiss – from me. How can you be so lazy with your own son?

As she straightened the duvet and smoothed the school shirt hanging on the chair, she heard the door bell.

'See you tomorrow, Mum.'

'Yes. Goodnight, love, sleep tight.'

Loud murmurings from the hall, and hearty laughter. Joanna leaned against the cool tiles in the bathroom and breathed in her own rich perfume. Her body still glowed from her early evening bath; she felt fragrant, fresh. I wish I could stay up here with my son, or alone, and quietly read away the evening.

'Jo – they're here.'

'Coming.'

The cigar smoke curled upwards past the deep browns of the Laura Ashley curtains and hung in swathes around the dimmed lights.

'That was delightful, Joanna. You really are an excellent cook. You're a lucky man, Charles.'

Brian exhaled bonhomie with his cigar and looked sleek, satisfied. Just ripe for the plucking – Charles would get his loan. Harriet's quiet tonight though. I must get a chance to talk to her.

'You all right now, Joanna? After that nasty knock. Just shows you how easily accidents can happen.'

'I'm fine thanks, Geoffrey. Perfectly recovered.'

'You slipped, didn't you? On the *Lancet* of all things?'

'Yes, I'm always telling James not to dash around the house without his slippers on, and I . . . well I was just off to bed, no shoes on, just stocking feet, and – of course I couldn't save myself. My arms were full of books and magazines actually, but even if they hadn't been, there was nothing I could do. My feet just shot from under me and wham . . . straight on to that dresser. My uncle said it was solid oak when he gave it to us – now I can believe it.'

'And how long were you in hospital?'

'Only two days, you know. After they'd X-rayed my skull

and given me the all clear. But it took me more than a week to get over it, I couldn't see straight, couldn't read, couldn't . . .

Charles stood up. 'Well, it's been most satisfactory to get things sorted out, hasn't it?'

'I quite agree.' Brian, like the others, took the hint and got up.

'No problems at all as far as we're concerned. A good investment for you is a good investment for us. You can count on us to put you right.'

As the last car drove out of earshot, Joanna emptied the ashtrays and straightened the cushions. Charles took her by the arm.

'Does it still bother you? Your head I mean?'

'Only sometimes. When it's damp I still get a twinge, a bit of a headache.'

'It won't happen again, you know, Jo. I promise you it won't happen again. I know I've got an awful temper, but it won't happen again.'

Until the next time. And who can a doctor's wife turn to? They don't have fitted carpets at Women's Aid, or gin . . .

As she switched off the light in the hall, Joanna again remembered the blood, *her* blood on the parquet floor . . .

'Please get the ambulance. For God's sake, Charles. I won't tell them. I'll say I slipped . . . but for pity's sake . . . get the ambulance.'

I wonder if his other patients have to plead with him when they need to go to hospital.

'Do you want to read?'

'No thanks. I'll go straight to sleep tonight. Early clinic tomorrow. You all right?'

'Yes, fine thanks. I've just got a bit of a headache.'

Charles twisted towards her, laid his arm on hers. 'It makes me feel guilty. You know I never *mean* to harm you. If we could just try a bit harder . . . if we . . .'

'I'm tired, Charles. Goodnight.'

I never could understand women who stayed with men who hit them. I still can't.

A Respectable Woman

Kate Chopin

Mrs Baroda was a little provoked to learn that her husband expected his friend, Gouvernail, up to spend a week or two on the plantation.

They had entertained a good deal during the winter; much of the time had also been passed in New Orleans in various forms of mild dissipation. She was looking forward to a period of unbroken rest, now, and undisturbed tête-à-tête with her husband, when he informed her that Gouvernail was coming up to stay a week or two.

This was a man she had heard much of but never seen. He had been her husband's college friend; was now a journalist, and in no sense a society man or 'man about town', which were, perhaps, some of the reasons she had never met him. But she had unconsciously formed an image of him in her mind. She pictured him tall, slim, cynical; with eye-glasses, and his hands in his pockets; and she did not like him. Gouvernail was slim enough, but he wasn't very tall nor very cynical; neither did he wear eye-glasses nor carry his hands in his pockets. And she rather liked him when he first presented himself.

But why she liked him she could not explain satisfactorily to herself when she partly attempted to do so. She could discover in him none of those brilliant and promising traits which Gaston, her husband, had often assured her that he possessed. On the contrary, he sat rather mute and receptive before her chatty eagerness to make him feel at home and in face of Gaston's frank and wordy hospitality. His manner was as courteous toward her as the most exacting woman could require; but he made no direct appeal to her approval or even esteem.

Once settled at the plantation he seemed to like to sit upon the wide portico in the shade of one of the big Corinthian pillars, smoking his cigar lazily and listening attentively to Gaston's experience as a sugar planter.

'This is what I call living,' he would utter with deep satisfaction, as the air that swept across the sugar field caressed him with its warm and scented velvety touch. It pleased him also to get on familiar terms with the big dogs that came about him, rubbing themselves sociably against his legs. He did not care to fish, and displayed no eagerness to go out and kill grosbecs when Gaston proposed doing so.

Gouvernail's personality puzzled Mrs Baroda, but she liked him. Indeed, he was a lovable, inoffensive fellow. After a few days, when she could understand him no better than at first, she gave over being puzzled and remained piqued. In this mood she left her husband and her guest, for the most part, alone together. Then finding that Gouvernail took no manner of exception to her action, she imposed her society upon him, accompanying him in his idle strolls to the mill and walks along the batture. She persistently sought to penetrate the reserve in which he had unconsciously enveloped himself.

'When is he going – your friend?' she one day asked her husband. 'For my part, he tires me frightfully.'

'Not for a week yet, dear. I can't understand; he gives you no trouble.'

'No. I should like him better if he did; if he were more like others, and I had to plan somewhat for his comfort and enjoyment.'

Gaston took his wife's pretty face between his hands and looked tenderly and laughingly into her troubled eyes. They were making a bit of toilet sociably together in Mrs Baroda's dressing-room.

'You are full of surprises, ma belle,' he said to her. 'Even I can never count upon how you are going to act under given conditions.' He kissed her and turned to fasten his cravat before the mirror.

'Here you are,' he went on, 'taking poor Gouvernail seriously and making a commotion over him, the last thing he would desire or expect.'

'Commotion!' she hotly resented. 'Nonsense! How can you say such a thing? Commotion, indeed! But, you know, you said he was clever.'

'So he is. But the poor fellow is run down by overwork now. That's why I asked him here to take a rest.'

'You used to say he was a man of ideas,' she retorted, unconciliated. 'I expected him to be interesting, at least. I'm going to the city in the morning to have my spring gowns fitted. Let me know when Mr Gouvernail is gone; I shall be at my Aunt Octavie's.'

That night she went and sat alone upon a bench that stood beneath a live oak tree at the edge of the gravel walk.

She had never known her thoughts or her intentions to be so confused. She could gather nothing from them but the feeling of a distinct necessity to quit her home in the morning.

Mrs Baroda heard footsteps crunching the gravel; but could discern in the darkness only the approaching red point of a lighted cigar. She knew it was Gouvernail, for her husband did not smoke. She hoped to remain unnoticed, but her white gown revealed her to him. He threw away his cigar and seated himself upon the bench beside her, without a suspicion that she might object to his presence.

'Your husband told me to bring this to you, Mrs Baroda,' he said, handing her a filmy, white scarf with which she sometimes enveloped her head and shoulders. She accepted the scarf from him with a murmur of thanks, and let it lie in her lap.

He made some commonplace observation upon the baneful effect of the night air at that season. Then as his gaze reached out into the darkness, he murmured, half to himself:

> 'Night of south winds – night of the large few stars!
> Still nodding night – '

She made no reply to this apostrophe to the night, which indeed, was not addressed to her.

Gouvernail was in no sense a diffident man, for he was

not a self-conscious one. His periods of reserve were not constitutional, but the result of moods. Sitting there beside Mrs Baroda, his silence melted for the time.

He talked freely and intimately in a low, hesitating drawl that was not unpleasant to hear. He talked of the old college days when he and Gaston had been a good deal to each other; of the days of keen and blind ambitions and large intentions. Now there was left with him, at least, a philosophic acquiescence to the existing order – only a desire to be permitted to exist, with now and then a little whiff of genuine life, such as he was breathing now.

Her mind only vaguely grasped what he was saying. Her physical being was for the moment predominant. She was not thinking of his words, only drinking in the tones of his voice. She wanted to reach out her hand in the darkness and touch him with the sensitive tips of her fingers upon the face or the lips. She wanted to draw close to him and whisper against his cheek – she did not care what – as she might have done if she had not been a respectable woman.

The stronger the impulse grew to bring herself near him, the further, in fact, did she draw away from him. As soon as she could do so without an appearance of too great rudeness, she rose and left him there alone.

Before she reached the house, Gouvernail had lighted a fresh cigar and ended his apostrophe to the night.

Mrs Baroda was greatly tempted that night to tell her husband – who was also her friend – of this folly that had seized her. But she did not yield to the temptation. Beside being a respectable woman she was a very sensible one; and she knew there are some battles in life which a human being must fight alone.

When Gaston arose in the morning, his wife had already departed. She had taken an early morning train to the city. She did not return till Gouvernail was gone from under her roof.

There was some talk of having him back during the summer that followed. That is, Gaston greatly desired it; but this desire yielded to his wife's strenuous opposition.

However, before the year ended, she proposed, wholly from herself, to have Gouvernail visit them again. Her husband was surprised and delighted with the suggestion coming from her.

'I am glad, *chère amie*, to know that you have finally overcome your dislike for him; truly he did not deserve it.'

'Oh,' she told him, laughingly, after pressing a long, tender kiss upon his lips, 'I have overcome everything! You will see. This time I shall be very nice to him.'

Shopping for One

Anne Cassidy

'So what did you say?' Jean heard the blonde woman in front of her talking to her friend.

'Well,' the darker woman began, 'I said I'm not having that woman there. I don't see why I should. I mean I'm not being old fashioned but I don't see why I should have to put up with her at family occasions. After all . . .' Jean noticed the other woman giving an accompaniment of nods and head-shaking at the appropriate parts. They fell into silence and the queue moved forward a couple of steps.

Jean felt her patience beginning to itch. Looking into her wire basket she counted ten items. That meant she couldn't go through the quick till but simply had to wait behind elephantine shopping loads; giant bottles of coke crammed in beside twenty pound bags of potatoes and 'special offer' drums of bleach. Somewhere at the bottom, Jean thought, there was always a plastic carton of eggs or a see-through tray of tomatoes which fell casualty to the rest. There was nothing else for it – she'd just have to wait.

'After all,' the dark woman resumed her conversation, 'how would it look if she was there when I turned up?' Her friend shook her head slowly from side to side and ended with a quick nod.

Should she have got such a small size salad cream? Jean wasn't sure. She was sick of throwing away half-used bottles of stuff.

'He came back to you after all,' the blonde woman suddenly

said. Jean looked up quickly and immediately felt her cheeks flush. She bent over and began to rearrange the items in her shopping basket.

'On his hands and knees,' the dark woman spoke in a triumphant voice. 'Begged me take him back.'

She gritted her teeth together. Should she go and change it for a larger size? Jean looked behind and saw that she was hemmed in by three large trolleys. She'd lose her place in the queue. There was something so pitiful about buying small sizes of everything. It was as though everyone knew.

'You can always tell a person by their shopping,' was one of her mother's favourite maxims. She looked into her shopping basket: individual fruit pies, small salad cream, yoghurt, tomatoes, cat food and a chicken quarter.

'It was only for sex you know. He admitted as much to me when he came back,' the darker woman informed her friend. Her friend began to load her shopping onto the conveyor belt. The cashier, doing what looked like an in-depth study of a biro suddenly said, 'Make it out to J. Sainsbury PLC.' She was addressing a man who had been poised and waiting to write out a cheque for a few moments. His wife was loading what looked like a gross of fish fingers into a cardboard box marked 'Whiskas'. It was called a division of labour.

Jean looked again at her basket and began to feel the familiar feeling of regret that visited her from time to time. Hemmed in between family-sized cartons of cornflakes and giant packets of washing-powder, her individual yoghurt seemed to say it all. She looked up towards a plastic bookstand which stood beside the till. A slim glossy hard-back caught her eye. The words *Cooking for One* screamed out from the front cover. Think of all the oriental foods you can get into, her friend had said. He was so traditional after all. Nodding in agreement with her thoughts Jean found herself eye to eye with the blonde woman, who, obviously not prepared to tolerate nodding at anyone else, gave her a blank, hard look and handed her what looked like a black plastic ruler with the words 'Next customer please' printed on it in bold letters. She turned back to her friend. Jean put the ruler down on the conveyor belt.

She thought about their shopping trips, before, when they were together, which for some reason seemed to assume massive proportions considering there were only two of them. All that rushing round, he pushing the trolley dejectedly, she firing questions at him. Salmon? Toilet rolls? Coffee? Peas? She remembered he only liked the processed kind. It was all such a performance. Standing there holding her wire basket, embarrassed by its very emptiness, was like something out of a soap opera.

'Of course, we've had our ups and downs,' the dark woman continued, lazily passing a few items down to her friend who was now on to what looked like her fourth Marks and Spencer carrier bag.

Jean began to load her food onto the conveyor belt. She picked up the cookery book and felt the frustrations of indecision. It was only ninety pence but it seemed to define everything, to pinpoint her aloneness, to prescribe an empty future. She put it back in its place.

'So that's why I couldn't have her there you see,' the dark woman was summing up. She lowered her voice to a loud whisper which immediately alerted a larger audience. 'And anyway, when he settles back in, I'm sure we'll sort out the other business then.' The friends exchanged knowing expressions and the blonde woman got her purse out of a neat leather bag. She peeled off three ten pound notes and handed them to the cashier.

Jean opened her carrier bag ready for her shopping. She turned to watch the two women as they walked off, the blonde pushing the trolley and the other seemingly carrying on with her story.

The cashier was looking expectantly at her and Jean realised that she had totalled up. It was four pounds and eighty seven pence. She had the right money, it just meant sorting her change out. She had an inclination that the people behind her were becoming impatient. She noticed their stack of items all lined and waiting, it seemed, for starter's orders. Brown bread and peppers, olive oil and lentils and, in the centre, a stray packet of beefburgers.

She gave over her money and picked up her carrier bag. She felt a sense of relief to be away from the mass of people. She felt out of place, a non conformer, half a consumer unit.

Walking out of the door she wondered what she might have for tea. Possibly chicken she thought, with salad.

Walking towards her car she thought that she should have bought the cookery book after all. She suddenly felt much better in the fresh air. She'd buy it next week. And in future she'd buy a large salad cream. After all, what if people came round unexpectedly?

Sunday in the Park

Bel Kaufman

It was still warm in the late-afternoon sun, and the city noises came muffled through the trees in the park. She put her book down on the bench, removed her sunglasses, and sighed contentedly. Morton was reading the *Times Magazine* section, one arm flung around her shoulder; their three-year-old son, Larry, was playing in the sandbox: a faint breeze fanned her hair softly against her cheek. It was five-thirty of a Sunday afternoon, and the small playground, tucked away in a corner of the park, was all but deserted. The swings and seesaws stood motionless and abandoned, the slides were empty, and only in the sandbox two little boys squatted diligently side by side. *How good this is,* she thought, and almost smiled at her sense of well-being. They must go out in the sun more often; Morton was so city-pale, cooped up all week inside the grey factorylike university. She squeezed his arm affectionately and glanced at Larry, delighting in the pointed little face frowning in concentration over the tunnel he was digging. The other boy suddenly stood up and with a quick, deliberate swing of his chubby arm threw a spadeful of sand at Larry. It just missed his head. Larry continued digging; the boy remained standing, shovel raised, stolid and impassive.

'No, no, little boy.' She shook her finger at him, her eyes searching for the child's mother or nurse. 'We mustn't throw sand. It may get in someone's eyes and hurt. We must play nicely in the nice sandbox.' The boy looked at her in unblinking expectancy. He was about Larry's age but perhaps ten pounds heavier, a husky little boy with none of Larry's quickness and sensitivity in his face. Where was his mother? The only other people left in the playground were two women and a little girl on roller skates leaving now through the gate, and a man on a bench a few feet away. He was a big man, and he seemed to be taking up the whole bench as he held the Sunday comics close to his face. She supposed he was the child's father. He did not look up from his comics, but spat once deftly out of the corner of his mouth. She turned her eyes away.

At that moment, as swiftly as before, the fat little boy threw another spadeful of sand at Larry. This time some of it landed on his hair and forehead. Larry looked up at his mother, his mouth tentative; her expression would tell him whether to cry or not.

Her first instinct was to rush to her son, brush the sand out of his hair, and punish the other child, but she controlled it. She always said that she wanted Larry to learn to fight his own battles.

'Don't *do* that, little boy,' she said sharply, leaning forward on the bench. 'You mustn't throw sand!'

The man on the bench moved his mouth as if to spit again, but instead he spoke. He did not look at her, but at the boy only.

'You go right ahead, Joe,' he said loudly. 'Throw all you want. This here is a *public* sandbox.'

She felt a sudden weakness in her knees as she glanced at Morton. He had become aware of what was happening. He put his *Times* down carefully on his lap and turned his fine, lean face toward the man, smiling the shy, apologetic smile he might have offered a student in pointing out an error in his thinking. When he spoke to the man, it was with his usual reasonableness.

'You're quite right,' he said pleasantly, 'but just because this is a public place . . .'

The man lowered his funnies and looked at Morton. He looked at him from head to foot, slowly and deliberately. 'Yeah?' His insolent voice was edged with menace. 'My kid's got just as good right here as yours, and if he feels like throwing sand, he'll throw it, and if you don't like it, you can take your kid the hell out of here.'

The children were listening, their eyes and mouths wide

open, their spades forgotten in small fists. She noticed the muscle in Morton's jaw tighten. He was rarely angry; he seldom lost his temper. She was suffused with a tenderness for her husband and an impotent rage against the man for involving him in a situation so alien and so distasteful to him.

'Now, just a minute,' Morton said courteously, 'you must realize . . .'

'Aw, shut up,' said the man.

Her heart began to pound. Morton half rose; the *Times* slid to the ground. Slowly the other man stood up. He took a couple of steps toward Morton, then stopped. He flexed his great arms, waiting. She pressed her trembling knees together. Would there be violence, fighting? How dreadful, how incredible. . . . She must do something, stop them, call for help. She wanted to put her hand on her husband's sleeve, to pull him down, but for some reason she didn't.

Morton adjusted his glasses. He was very pale. 'This is ridiculous,' he said unevenly. 'I must ask you . . .'

'Oh, yeah?' said the man. He stood with his legs spread apart, rocking a little, looking at Morton with utter scorn. 'You and who else?'

For a moment the two men looked at each other nakedly. Then Morton turned his back on the man and said quietly, 'Come on, let's get out of here.' He walked awkwardly, almost limping with self-consciousness, to the sandbox. He stooped and lifted Larry and his shovel out.

At once Larry came to life; his face lost its rapt expression and he began to kick and cry. 'I don't *want* to go home, I want to play better, I don't *want* any supper, I don't *like* supper. . .' It became a chant as they walked, pulling their child between them, his feet dragging on the ground. In order to get to the exit gate they had to pass the bench where the man sat sprawling again. She was careful not to look at him. With all the dignity she could summon, she pulled Larry's sandy, perspiring little hand, while Morton pulled the other. Slowly and with head high she walked with her husband and child out of the playground.

Her first feeling was one of relief that a fight had been avoided, that no one was hurt. Yet beneath it there was a layer of something else, something heavy and inescapable. She sensed that it was more than just an unpleasant incident, more than a defeat of reason by force. She felt dimly it had something to do with her and Morton, something acutely personal, familiar, and important.

Suddenly Morton spoke. 'It wouldn't have proved anything.'

'What?' she asked.

'A fight. It wouldn't have proved anything beyond the fact that he's bigger than I am.'

'Of course,' she said.

'The only possible outcome,' he continued reasonably, 'would have been – what? My glasses broken, perhaps a tooth or two replaced, a couple of days' work missed – and for what? For justice? For truth?'

'Of course,' she repeated. She quickened her step. She wanted only to get home and to busy herself with her familiar tasks; perhaps then the feeling, glued like heavy plaster on her heart, would be gone. *Of all the stupid, despicable bullies,* she thought, pulling harder on Larry's hand. The child was still crying. Always before she had felt a tender pity for his defenceless little body, the frail arms, the narrow shoulders with sharp, winglike shoulder blades, the thin and unsure legs, but now her mouth tightened in resentment.

'Stop crying,' she said sharply. 'I'm ashamed of you!' She felt as if all three of them were tracking mud along the street. The child cried louder.

If there had been an issue involved, she thought, *if there had been something to fight for. . . . But what else could he possibly have done? Allow himself to be beaten? Attempt to educate the man? Call a policeman? 'Officer, there's a man in the park who won't stop his child from throwing sand on mine. . .'* The whole thing was as silly as that, and not worth thinking about.

'Can't you keep him quiet, for Pete's sake?' Morton asked irritably.

'What do you suppose I've been trying to do?' she said.

Larry pulled back, dragging his feet.

'If you can't discipline this child, I will,' Morton snapped, making a move toward the boy.

But her voice stopped him. She was shocked to hear it, thin and cold and penetrating with contempt. 'Indeed?' she heard herself say. 'You and who else?'

The Shelter

R.K. Narayan

The rain came down suddenly. The only shelter he could run to was the banyan tree on the roadside, with its huge trunk and the spreading boughs above. He watched, with detachment, the rain patter down with occasional sprays coming in his direction. He watched idly a mongrel trotting off, his coat completely wet, and a couple of buffaloes on the roadside eating cast-off banana leaves. He suddenly became aware of another person standing under the tree, beyond the curve of the tree trunk. A faint scent of flower wafted towards him, and he could not contain his curiosity; he edged along the tree trunk, and suddenly found himself face to face with her. His first reaction was to let out a loud 'Oh!' and he looked miserable and confused. The lady saw him and suppressed a scream. When he had recovered his composure, he said, 'Don't worry, I will go away.' It seemed a silly thing to say to one's wife after a long separation. He moved back to his previous spot away from her. But presently he came back to ask, 'What brought you here?'

He feared she might not reply, but she said, 'Rain.' 'Oh!' He tried to treat it as a joke and please her by laughing. 'It brought me also here,' he said, feeling idiotic. She said nothing in reply. The weather being an ever-obliging topic, he tried to cling to it desperately and said, 'Unexpected rain.' She gave no response to his remark and looked away. He tried to drag on the subject further. 'If I had had the slightest suspicion of its coming, I would have stayed indoors or brought my umbrella.' She ignored his statement completely. She might be deaf for all it mattered. He wanted to ask, Are your ears affected? but feared that she might feel irritated. She was capable of doing anything when upset. He had never suspected the strength of her feelings until that night of final crisis.

They had had several crises in their years of married life. Every other hour they expressed differing views on everything under the sun: every question precipitated a crisis, none too trivial to be ignored. It might be anything – whether to listen to Radio Ceylon or All India Radio, whether one should see an English picture or a Tamil one, whether jasmine smell might be termed too strong or otherwise, a rose could be termed gaudy or not, and so forth. Anything led to an argument and created tension, and effected a breach between the partners for a number of days, to be followed by a reconciliation and an excessive friendliness. In one such mood of reconciliation they had even drawn an instrument of friendship with elaborate clauses, and signed it before the gods in the *puja* room with a feeling that nothing would bother them again and that all their troubles were at an end. But it was short-lived and the very first clause of the contract, 'We shall never quarrel hereafter', was the first to be broken within twenty-four hours of signing the deed, and all the other clauses, which covered such possible causes of difference as household expenses, criticism of food, budget discussions, references to in-laws (on all of which elaborate understanding had been evolved), did not mean anything.

Now standing in the rain he felt happy that she was cornered. He had had no news of her after he had shut the door on her that night as it seemed so long ago. They had argued over the food as usual, she threatened to leave the home, and he said, 'Go ahead,' and held the door open while she had walked out into the night. He left the door unbolted for a long time in the belief that she would return, but she didn't.

'I didn't hope to see you again,' he ventured to say now and she answered, 'Did you think I would go and drown myself?' 'Yes, that I feared,' he said.

'Did you look for me in the nearby wells, or ponds?'

'Or the river?' he added. 'I didn't.'

'It would have surprised me if you had had so much concern.'

He said, 'You didn't drown yourself after all, how could you blame me for not looking for you?' He appealed to her pathetically. She nearly stamped her foot as she said, 'That only shows you have no heart.'

'You are very unreasonable,' he said.

'Oh, God, you have started giving a reading of my character. It is my ill fate that the rain should have come down just now and driven me over here.'

'On the contrary, I think it is a good rain. It has brought us together. May I now ask what you have been doing with yourself all this time?'

'Should I answer?' He detected in her voice a certain amount of concern and he felt flattered. Could he induce her to come back to him? The sentence almost formed itself on the tip of his tongue but he thrust it back. He merely asked, 'Aren't you concerned with my own lot? Don't you care to know what I have been doing with myself all these months?' She didn't reply. She simply watched the rain pouring down more than ever. The wind's direction suddenly changed and a gust flung a spray of water on her face. He treated it as an excuse to dash up to her with his kerchief. She recoiled from his approach. 'Don't bother about me,' she cried.

'You're getting wet. . .' A bough above shook a few drops on her hair. He pointed his finger at her anxiously and said, 'You are getting drenched unnecessarily. You could move down a little this way. If you like I will stand where you are.' He expected her to be touched by this solicitude. She merely replied, 'You need not worry about me.' She stood grimly looking at the rain as it churned up the road. 'Shall I dash up and bring an umbrella or a taxi?' he asked. She merely glared at him and turned away. He said something else on the same lines and she asked, 'Am I your toy?'

'Why do you say toy? I said no such thing.'

'You think you can pick me up when you like and throw me out when you feel that way. Only toys are treated thus.'

'I never told you to go away,' he said.

'I am not listening to any of that again,' she said.

'I am probably dying to say how sorry I am,' he began.

'May be, but go and say that to someone else.'

'I have no one else to say such things to,' he said.

'That is your trouble, is it?' she asked. 'That doesn't interest me.'

'Have you no heart?' he pleaded. 'When I say I am sorry, believe me. I am changed now.'

'So am I,' she said. 'I am not my old self now. I expect nothing in others and I am never disappointed,' she said.

'Won't you tell me what you are doing?' he pleaded. She shook her head. He said, 'Someone said that you were doing *harijan* work or some such thing. See how I am following your activities!' She said nothing in reply. He asked, 'Do you live all the time here or. . . ?' It was plain that he was trying to get her address. She threw a glance at the rain, and then looked at him sourly. He said, 'Well, I didn't order the rain anyway. We have got to face it together.'

'Not necessarily. Nothing can hold me thus,' she said, and suddenly dashed into the rain and broke into a run. He cried after her, 'Wait, wait. I promise not to talk. Come back, don't get drenched,' but she was off, vanishing beyond the curtain of raindrops.

puja Hindu worship
harijan people of low caste

The Unseeing Eye

Hanan Al-Shaykh

The old man stood there at a loss, his sunken eyes staring at the man seated behind the table. Raising his hand, he wiped the sweat from his forehead and heavily wrinkled face. He didn't use the traditional kerchief and headband though he could feel the sweat running down his temples and neck, and he gave no reply to the man seated behind the table who went on asking him, 'Why did you go in opening all the doors of the wards looking for your wife? Why didn't you come directly to Enquiries?' The old man kept silent. Why, though, was the man seated behind the table continuing to open one drawer after another? His eyes busy watching him, he said, 'I came here the day before yesterday wanting the hospital and looking for the mother of my children.'

The man seated behind the table muttered irritably, blaming himself for not having ever learnt how to ask the right questions, how to get a conversation going, and why it was that his questions, full of explanations, and sometimes of annoyance, weren't effective. He puffed at his cigarette as he enquired in exasperation, 'What's your wife's name?' The old man at once replied, 'Zeinab Mohamed.' The man seated behind the table began flipping through the pages of the thick ledger; each time he turned over a page there was a loud noise that was heard by everyone sitting in the waiting-room. He went on flipping through the pages of his ledger, pursing his lips listlessly, then nervously, as he kept bringing the ledger close to his face until finally he said, 'Your wife came in here the day before yesterday?' The old man in relief at once answered, 'Yes, sir, when her heart came to a stop.' Once again irritated, the man behind the table mumbled to himself, 'Had her heart stopped she wouldn't be here, neither would you.' With his eyes still on the ledger, he said, 'She's in Ward 4, but it's not permitted for you to enter her ward because there are other women there.' Yawning, he called to the nurse leaning against the wall. She came forward, in her hand a paper cup from which she was drinking. Motioning with his head to the man, he said, 'Ward Number 4 – Zeinab Mohamed.' The nurse walked ahead, without raising her mouth from the cup. The old man asked himself how it was that this woman worked in a hospital that was crammed with men, even though she spoke Arabic. Having arrived at the ward, the nurse left him outside after telling him to wait; then, after a while, she came out and said to him, 'There are two women called Zeinab Mohamed. One of them, though, has only one eye. Which one is your wife so that I can call her?'

The old man was thrown into confusion. One eye? How am I to know? He tried to recall what his wife Zeinab looked like, with her long gown and black headdress, the veil, and sometimes the black covering enveloping her face and sometimes removed and lying on her neck. He could picture her as she walked and sat, chewing a morsel and then taking it out of her mouth so as to place it in that of her first-born. Her children. One eye. How am I to know? He could picture her stretched out on the bed, her eyes closed. The old man was thrown into confusion and found himself saying, 'When I call her she'll know my voice.' The nurse doubted whether he was in fact visiting his wife; however, giving him another glance, she laughed at her suspicions and asked him, 'How long have the two of you been married?' Again he was confused as he said, 'Allah knows best – thirty, forty years. . .'

The Hitch-hiker

Francis Greig

It had been touch and go whether Carole Phillips would reach the London main-line station in time to catch the last train. She had worked very late that night, preparing a report on the small department she managed in the London office of a textile manufacturer; and, since she would be too late and too tired to cook when she arrived home, had gone to a small restaurant for a salad before looking for a taxi to take her to the station.

The service at the restaurant had been slow and when she left the place a slight drizzle had begun to fall: enough to make taxis irritatingly scarce. Finally, though, she flagged one down and sat on the edge of her seat as it dragged through the traffic towards the station. She made the train with seconds to spare and fell against the buttoned upholstery, recovering slowly from her sprint through the station concourse.

During the seventy-minute trip to the Home Counties town where she lived, she looked up from her book now and then to peer out of the window into the darkness. The rain had quickened. Heavy drops, blown into a spread of wet lace, hung on the glass. Beyond, she could see the black shadows of trees alongside the line stirring in the wind; and behind the trees the indistinct, sodden fields lit along their edges by the lights from the carriages. She reflected that even the tamest countryside can seem intimidating at night: and especially in bad weather. Out there in the blackness, predators were closing in on their prey – ruthlessly, silently. In those apparently empty fields, sudden attacks were taking place; there were tiny, unheard screams of pain; there was blood and violent death, the killer standing above its victim as the little corpse still quivered in its grip. This late at night, the normally tolerable trip could seem endless.

By the time she reached her destination, the weather had become wild. The rain had thinned, but was carried almost horizontally by a harsh, cold wind that buffeted her as she struggled along the platform. She was the only passenger to alight. Her heeltaps rang on the flagstones, seeming to sing, like asdic, as if they were finding a resonance below the surface. She always felt slightly at risk when coming home on the last train – silly, of course; a hangover from childhood fears of the dark, of the bogeyman, of the imagined figure at the top of the stairs. Even so, she never felt quite safe until she had crossed the car-park and (feeling a bit foolish) locked herself into the car before starting off.

As usual, this late at night, there was no one on duty to take her ticket. A light burned dimly in one of the station rooms, but whoever was in there either hadn't noticed that a passenger had got off the train, or didn't care. She pushed her season-ticket back into her pocket and took out her car keys.

She had arrived at the station that morning with only a few minutes to spare: cutting things fine is a characteristic of the practised commuter. So her car had been parked among the furthest from the entrance, although now it was the only vehicle left there beneath the row of tossing yew trees that bordered the fence.

The car-park was no more than a large, cordoned-off area of bare earth, rutted and strewn with cinders for drainage – unlit and far from the sparse street-lamps lining the country road by the station approach. She crossed the sixty yards or so of rough ground at a fast pace, her coat flapping in the wind. Once she stumbled in a deep rut and almost loosed her hold on the car keys – that would have been a disaster, she thought, since it was too dark to see more than a few feet ahead. She knew exactly where the car was, though, and walked unfalteringly to it. As she put the key in the lock, she heard a quiet voice from out of the blackness directly behind her.

For a second her heart seemed to stop entirely. Then her brain began to function, offering reassurance: it had been a woman's voice. Even so, she turned to face the voice's owner with fear curdling in her stomach; but as the person came a little closer, she relaxed. A woman stood there, dressed rather shabbily in a worn top-coat and a felt hat. Her hair was grey, she was clearly in late-middle age, and she seemed to be upset.

'Excuse me, Miss,' she repeated the words that the girl had first heard.

'What's wrong?' Clearly something must be wrong. Why else would this old dear be standing in a station car-park at midnight enduring a half-gale?

'Can you help me? It's so silly. I arranged for a taxi to meet me from my train and it's not here. I thought your car might be it and that the driver would come back, but I've been waiting for ages. Are you going towards town?'

'Yes. I'm going into the town.' The girl began to feel distinctly sorry for the old lady. To be stuck out at the station – a four-mile bus or cab ride from the town – waiting for transport that obviously wasn't going to come almost put her in the category of distressed gentleperson. 'Where do you live?'

'Well, it's on that road – almost in the town itself. You could very nearly drop me at my door without going out of your way. Would you mind?'

The girl unlocked the car and got in, then lifted the catch on the passenger-door to admit the old lady. When they were both settled, the girl leaned over and opened the glove-compartment on the passenger's side. She kept a wooden clothes-peg in there: her unscientific but effective method for keeping the erratic choke out long enough to get the car going. She had just retrieved the peg, when she happened to glance down. She froze. The illumination from the glove-compartment revealed that the backs of her passenger's hands – which were neatly folded in her lap – were covered in a thick growth of dark hairs!

The girl's mind screamed at her: *It's a man! Oh, my God, it's a man!* Somehow, she managed to remain outwardly calm, fiddling with this or that control while her brain raced, desperately trying to improvise an escape. By some means, she had to get the person out of the car.

Without pegging the choke back, she turned the ignition key, knowing that the car wouldn't start. Three or four times she made a show of doing this, pretending to get more annoyed. Hoping that her voice wouldn't quaver, she said, 'Oh dear! It does this sometimes. Usually, I have to get a push.' Then she turned the key twice more, to no effect.

'Damn!' She chewed her lip as if searching for a solution. 'Look, it's an awful thing to ask, but I don't see how else we're going to get the wretched car started. We're on a bit of a hill here. If you could just give it a tiny push to start it off, it'll roll down the slope and I can get the engine going. Would you?'

Somewhat to her surprise, her passenger agreed. Maybe the light in the station – impossibly far as a refuge, but close enough to make a potential attacker feel uneasy – had influenced the matter. Anyway, the girl waited, breathlessly, as the passenger-door closed and the figure went around to the back of the car. Instantly, she snapped down the inside locks, jammed the peg behind the choke-rod, started the car, roared across the car-park, along the station approach and on to the road.

After a mile or so, the mad fluttering of the girl's heart slowed. The whole incident seemed dream-like. She could hardly believe it had really happened – though if she needed to assure herself that it had, she had the evidence of the handbag that the old lady had left on the floor of the car when she got out. In fact, it may have been the handbag that first caused the girl to wonder whether she mightn't have acted rather hastily. Had she perhaps just swept out of the car-park leaving behind a thoroughly confused old lady who simply happened to have rather hairy hands? After all, some women were unlucky that way and only the young would bother to do something about the condition. More than that, the light from the glove-compartment might have made the hairiness look worse than it was. What evidence did she have? Almost none. She was aware, though, that her natural nervousness, her slight fear of the dark and the wild weather might have prompted her to act stupidly. If she *had* made a mistake, then she had driven off with the poor woman's handbag. But still she remembered those *very* hairy hands!

By the time she reached town, she was in a terrible

quandary about the whole incident. Had she just survived an encounter with a homicidal maniac or had her irrational fear led her to act in a terribly unkind manner? Either way, she decided, her best course of action was to go to the local police station. The person she had just abandoned would need to be either rescued or investigated.

As she told her story to the sergeant on duty, she became increasingly sure in her own mind that she had acted cruelly and stupidly. It *had* been an old lady; hairy hands were no sign of malice; and she had left her out there at the station with no means of getting home.

She said as much to the sergeant, who agreed that it was probably the case. 'I'll send someone out there,' he told the girl. 'In the meantime, we'd better have a look in her handbag to find out who she is in case she's left the station.'

Together, they went out to the car. The girl produced the bag – a large soft-leather affair with a swivel clasp – and handed it to the sergeant, who snapped open the clasp and held the bag open so that they could both see what it held.

The sergeant's exclamation was followed by a small shriek from the girl; she staggered slightly and seemed about to faint, so that the policeman had to support her by an arm. The shaft of the axe had been sawn short so that it would fit into the bag. It was the only thing in there, and the honed cutting edge shone along its bevelled length in the white lamp-light.

Faces

Dennis Hamley

The road was straight. The night was cold. The sky was clear. The moon shone pale. The tall trees by the side of the road cast narrow shadows across it, so that the man who ran, panting and frightened, had the strange impression that he was toiling up a long flight of stairs.

His heartbeats sounded like muffled drums in his ears, not quite in rhythm with his echoing feet. Sweat poured into his eyes, though the night was bitterly cold.

From time to time, a car would pass him going the other way. Its headlights would search him out and then ignore him: the lowering in pitch of the engine noise as it swept past him sounded like a contemptuous dismissal. Every now and then, without pausing in his stride, the man would steal a look behind him, half fearfully, half hopefully. And all the while, the desperation and sick dread mounted in his mind.

How long had he been running? It seemed as though he had been pounding breathlessly on, one foot in front of the other, since the moment he was born. Yet could he have run much more than a mile? And how many miles more did he have still to run?

He snatched another look behind him. Far down the road he saw what looked like two pale eyes. He turned round – though he kept running, so he was now actually stumbling backwards. The eyes drew nearer. They were the headlights of a car – but not with the piercing brightness of halogen bulbs on main beam. The car drew nearer. Suddenly almost crazed with relief, the man stepped into its path, waving his arms and hardly caring for his safety. The car drew to a halt: the lights close to made the man blink.

He walked to the passenger door and the driver leant across to open it for him. The car was old: a magnificent black Daimler of pre-war vintage. For the moment, the man cared nothing for this. It was a car, and a car meant speed and escape.

'For God's sake take me to the next town,' he gasped.

The driver sat back, calm and almost statuesque, in his capacious leather-upholstered seat. In the moonlight the man could see he wore a very expensive overcoat, a hat pulled low over his head and a woollen scarf. His face was in darkness, but from the depths of the scarf came a level, smooth, mellifluous voice.

'Certainly,' he said.

The panting man climbed over the running board and into the car. He settled into the front passenger seat and began to breathe more easily. For some minutes the journey proceeded quietly. The muffled figure behind the wheel drove speedily along the straight, dark road. The old but perfect car hummed regally along. Its new passenger regained his breath completely and with it some of his composure.

At length, the driver spoke. The first impression of calm evenness in his voice was confirmed.

'Tell me, sir – for indeed I could not help but notice the state you were in when I stopped for you – the cause of your perturbation.'

The passenger gulped. For a moment it seemed as though he was unwilling to say anything at all about his experiences. Then – in the warm, steadily-driven car, insulated from the evils of the dark night outside, he relaxed.

'Very well,' he said.

And then he commenced his story.

'My own car,' he said, 'broke down about three miles back along the road. The useless thing was completely dead: I tinkered around with what tools I had but it was hopeless. I needed help. I realised I was miles from anywhere on a lonely road I had never seen before. What could I do? I just had to lock the car up and walk. Perhaps, I reasoned, there might be a house nearby where perhaps I could get help – or at least make a telephone call.

'I must have walked for well over a mile without seing any sign of life. I almost decided to go back and sleep in the car till morning. How I wish I had.'

He paused for a moment.

'Go on,' the driver said.

'Then I saw a house standing back from the road. The wrought-iron gates were open: a weedy, gravelled drive led up to a dark front door. It was a large house with a high-pitched roof and leaded windows with small panes. There were no lights on: it seemed deserted. But the front gate was open, so perhaps it was worth calling. Somebody might be there to help me. So I scrunched up the gravel drive to the front door, saw a bell-pull and, naturally enough, pulled it.

'Almost before the bell started jangling through the house, the front door opened. The surprise of that – almost as if whoever was behind the door had been waiting for the bell to ring – took my breath away.

'In the doorway stood a figure. I had a definite impression that it was a woman, though she was carefully shading the candle she held so that nothing of her was revealed but only the bare floorboards and walls of the entrance hall in which she stood.

'"Come inside," she said.

'Her voice was low and resonant in the empty hall. She turned away from me, beckoning as she did so. Without questioning my action at all, I followed her. She led me up uncarpeted stairs and paused on the landing. The candle was still the only source of light.

'In the shadows, I could make out several closed doors. But one door – I could tell by a very faint light stretching vertically from lintel to floor – was open. A voice called out from behind it. It was a man's voice – and it too had a clarity and sweetness of tone that rings in my ears even now.

'"Who is it, my dear?"

'The woman answered with words that should have chilled my heart.

'"It is he whom we have expected."

'Yes, I know I should have turned tail and run away then –

away from that accursed place for ever. But I did not. For the feeling still uppermost in me was relief at having found help and shelter with people who sounded so kind.

'The woman led me to the open door. I saw then where the light had come from. The moon was now fully up and its cold light poured in through the curtainless, leaded windows opposite me. Between me and the window was a large table with what looked to be an oil-lamp placed on it. And behind the table was the shape of a man, standing.

'The woman moved away from me to stand beside him.

'For a moment, there was complete silence and stillness. I waited for something to happen, something more to be said.

'Then the man leant forward. There was a scratch, a sudden flare from a match. He had lit the lamp. A warm, yellow light threw shadows round the room. I blinked in sudden surprise: I had become used to semi-darkness. So I looked round at this bare room, at the beams of the ceiling, the great oak table, the heavy, carved chairs pushed back against the walls. And I looked at my new companions, now that I had light to see them with.

'And then my face froze into horror and my voice formed itself into a wordless scream.

'For the faces of both the man and the woman were the same. No mouth. No nose. No eyes. They were smooth, bare, featureless – as eggs.'

Here the storyteller paused and shuddered, as if the memory was too much for him. The driver said nothing – the Daimler purred on its way. The storyteller took a deep breath and continued.

'Without thinking twice, I turned and ran. I swept through the doorway, almost fell down the stairs in my headlong rush, fought desperately to push the front door open till I remembered it opened inward, stumbled along the gravel drive and out again on to the road. I listened for footsteps behind me: I heard none. I took one last look at the house as I passed the open gates: at the lighted window of that upstairs room I could see the two human-seeming silhouettes surveying my departure.

'On I ran, the way I had been going before, desperate for help, for consolation, for assurance that I had been merely the victim of a mistake, a practical joke, a hallucination, perhaps a nightmare. And then, as if in answer to a prayer, you stop for me, and I am back in the world of normality.'

He gave a sigh of relief and satisfaction and settled comfortably and confidently back in the soft leather seat as the Daimler sped smoothly onward.

The driver's hands stayed calmly on the steering wheel. For almost the first time since the passenger had commenced his story, he spoke.

'You say their faces had no features on them. Were they, in fact, quite blank?'

'Yes,' said the passenger.

The driver turned to his companion and with his left hand removed his scarf.

'You mean,' he said, 'like this?'

No mouth. No nose. No eyes. A face as blank and smooth and featureless as an egg.

Hobbyist

Fredric Brown

'I heard a rumour,' Sangstrom said, 'to the effect that you – ' He turned his head and looked about him to make absolutely sure that he and the druggist were alone in the tiny prescription pharmacy. The druggist was a gnomelike gnarled little man who could have been any age from fifty to a hundred. They were alone, but Sangstrom dropped his voice just the same. ' – to the effect that you have a completely undetectable poison.'

The druggist nodded. He came around the counter and locked the front door of the shop, then walked toward a doorway behind the counter. 'I was about to take a coffee break,' he said. 'Come with me and have a cup.'

Sangstrom followed him around the counter and through the doorway to a back room ringed by shelves of bottles from floor to ceiling. The druggist plugged in an electric percolator, found two cups and put them on a table that had a chair on either side of it. He motioned Sangstrom to one of the chairs and took the other himself. 'Now,' he said. 'Tell me. Whom do you want to kill, and why?'

'Does it matter?' Sangstrom asked. 'Isn't it enough that I pay for – '

The druggist interrupted him with an upraised hand. 'Yes, it matters. I must be convinced that you deserve what I can give you. Otherwise – ' He shrugged.

'All right,' Sangstrom said. 'The *whom* is my wife. The *why* – ' He started the long story. Before he had quite finished, the percolator had finished its task and the druggist briefly interrupted to get the coffee for them. Sangstrom finished his story.

The little druggist nodded. 'Yes, I occasionally dispense an undetectable poison. I do so freely; I do not charge for it, if I think the case is deserving. I have helped many murderers.'

'Fine,' Sangstrom said. 'Please give it to me, then.'

The druggist smiled at him. 'I already have. By the time the coffee was ready I had decided that you deserved it. It was, as I said, free. But there is a price for the antidote.'

Sangstrom turned pale. But he had anticipated – not this, but the possibility of a double-cross or some form of blackmail. He pulled a pistol from his pocket.

The little druggist chuckled. 'You daren't use that. Can you find the antidote' – he waved at the shelves – 'among those thousands of bottles? Or would you find a faster more virulent poison? Or if you think I'm bluffing, that you are not really poisoned, go ahead and shoot. You'll know the answer within three hours when the poison starts to work.'

'How much for the antidote?' Sangstrom growled.

'Quite reasonable. A thousand dollars. After all, a man must live. Even if his hobby is preventing murders, there's no reason why he shouldn't make money at it, is there?'

Sangstrom growled and put the pistol down, but within reach, and took out his wallet. Maybe after he had the antidote, he'd still use that pistol. He counted out a thousand dollars in hundred-dollar bills and put it on the table.

The druggist made no immediate move to pick it up. He said: 'And one other thing – for your wife's safety and mine. You will write a confession of your intention – your former intention, I trust – to murder your wife. Then you will wait till I go out and mail it to a friend of mine on the homicide detail. He'll keep it as evidence in case you ever *do* decide to kill your wife. Or me, for that matter.

'When that is in the mail it will be safe for me to return here and give you the antidote. I'll get you paper and pen . . .

'Oh, one other thing – although I do not absolutely insist on it. Please help spread the word about my undetectable poison, will you? One never knows, Mr Sangstrom. The life you save, if you have any enemies, just might be your own.'

Doctor's Orders

John F. Suter

The pain. The pain is everywhere. No, not everywhere, but I throb in the places where there is no real pain. And now it is only an ache and an exhaustion, but it seems as if there is no time, no space, nothing but this. But I am a little stronger than I was. So little. But I am stronger. I have to get well. I intend to get well. I will get well.

'Mr Shaw, I think she'll come out of it all right. As you know, it was either your wife or the baby, for a while. But she's improved, I assure you. Of course, there will always be that weakness which we can't correct.'

'I understand. Just to have her well again is all I care about.'

I had better open my eyes. Jeff isn't here. I can't sense him. But I can stand the white room now. I no longer have a wish to die. Even though he didn't live. I could grieve and grieve and grieve, and I wanted to when Jeff first told me. But there is no strength in that sort of grief. I will get well.

'You did tell her that the baby died?'

'Yes, Doctor. It was hard for her to take at first. Very hard. Then I told her that it had been a boy. That pleased her, in spite of – of what happened.'

There. The world is back. So much sunshine in the room. So many flowers. I wonder if Jeff –

'Did you tell her that the child is already buried?'

'Not yet. If you're sure that she's stronger, I'll tell her today.'

'You don't think she'll hold it against you for going ahead with the funeral, Mr Shaw?'

'Jessie is very level-headed, Doctor. She'll understand that we couldn't wait. And – if you don't think it's out of style to say so – we love each other.'

I'm sure Jeff has done whatever is best. If only it – he – had lived until I could have seen him . . . How long have I been here? Where is Jeff? Is he being sensible, as I begged him to be? Is he at work, so that he won't endanger his job, the job that's so important to him? Oh, I do love him, and I do so want to give him fine children.

'Perhaps, then, Mr Shaw, it would be better for you to tell her the rest of it than for me to do it. It might be easier for her to believe someone who loves her. Sometimes the patient thinks the doctor doesn't know as much as she herself does.'

'That part won't be easy.'

I hope the children will look like Jeff. I'm not ugly, but I'm so – plain. Jeff has the looks for us both. That's one of the reasons they all said he was only after my money. But he's refused to let me help him. He's independent. He keeps working hard managing the sporting-goods department, when neither of us would ever have to work again, if we didn't want to. I must get well, for his sake. I will get well.

'Easy or hard, Mr Shaw, it has to be done. Someone has to tell her. It will come best from you. She must never try to have a child again. Never. It will kill her. Make no mistake about it – having another child will kill her.'

'I'll take the responsibility, Doctor. You needn't say a thing to her. I think I can convince her. Perhaps I can even persuade her to move away for a while, so that old associations won't keep haunting her.'

I'm glad that I made my will in Jeff's favour before I came

to the hospital. He doesn't know about it, and it wasn't necessary, as it turned out. But I'm glad. He's been so good to me that now I'm sure of him . . .

The door swung inwards, silently. She turned her head, slowly, and a tired smile crept across her white face. A tall young man with crinkled blond hair was in the doorway.

'Jeff.'

He was at her bedside, kissing her palm. 'Jessie.'

When they both could speak, she gripped his fingers. 'Jeff, I've been lying here thinking. Everybody has troubles of some kind or other. We can overcome this. I'm going to get strong, fast. Then we're going to have another baby, just as quickly as we can. Aren't we?'

He smiled proudly. The truth was exactly the right answer. 'We certainly are, sweetheart. We certainly are.'

Mr Lupescu

Anthony Boucher

The teacups rattled and flames flickered over the logs.

'Alan, I *do* wish you could do something about Bobby.'

'Isn't that rather Robert's place?'

'Oh, you know *Robert*. He's so busy doing good in nice abstract ways with committees in them.'

'And headlines.'

'He can't be bothered with things like Mr Lupescu. After all, Bobby's only his *son*.'

'And yours, Marjorie.'

'And mine. But things like this take a *man*, Alan.'

The room was warm and peaceful; Alan stretched his long legs by the fire and felt domestic. Marjorie was soothing even when she fretted. The firelight did things to her hair and the curve of her blouse.

A small whirlwind entered at high velocity and stopped only when Marjorie said, 'Bob-*by*! Say hello nicely to Uncle Alan.'

Bobby said hello and stood tentatively on one foot.

'Alan . . .' Marjorie prompted.

Alan sat upright and tried to look paternal. 'Well, Bobby,' he said. 'And where are you off to in such a hurry?'

'See Mr Lupescu, 'f course. He usually comes afternoons.'

'Your mother's been telling me about Mr Lupescu. He must be quite a person.'

'Oh, gee, I'll say he is, Uncle Alan. He's got a great big red nose and red gloves and red eyes – not like when you've been crying but really red like yours 're brown – and little red wings that twitch, only he can't fly with them cause they're ruddermentary he says. And he talks like – oh, gee, I can't do it, but he's swell, he is.'

'Lupescu's a funny name for a fairy godfather, isn't it, Bobby?'

'Why? Mr Lupescu always says why do all the fairies have to be Irish because it takes all kinds, doesn't it?'

'Alan!' Marjorie said. 'I don't see that you're doing a *bit* of good. You talk to him seriously like that and you simply make him think it *is* serious. And you *do* know better, don't you, Bobby? You're just joking with us.'

'Joking? About *Mr Lupescu*?'

'Marjorie, you don't – listen, Bobby. Your mother didn't mean to insult you or Mr Lupescu. She just doesn't believe in what she's never seen, and you can't blame her. Now supposing you took her and me out in the garden and we could all see Mr Lupescu. Wouldn't that be fun?'

'Uh, uh.' Bobby shook his head gravely. 'Not for Mr Lupescu. He doesn't like people. Only little boys. And he says if I ever bring people to see him then he'll let Gorgo get me. G'bye now.' And the whirlwind departed.

Marjorie sighed. 'At least thank heavens for Gorgo. I never can get a very clear picture out of Bobby, but he says Mr Lupescu tells the most *terrible* things about him. And if there's any trouble about vegetables or brushing teeth all I have to say is *Gorgo* and hey presto!'

Alan rose. 'I don't think you need worry, Marjorie. Mr Lupescu seems to do more good than harm, and an active imagination is no curse to a child.'

'You haven't *lived* with Mr Lupescu.'

'To live in a house like this, I'd chance it,' Alan laughed. 'But please forgive me now – back to the cottage and the typewriter. Seriously, why don't you ask Robert to talk with him?'

Marjorie spread her hands helplessly.

'I know. I'm always the one to assume responsibilities. And yet you married Robert.'

Marjorie laughed. 'I don't know. Somehow there's something *about* Robert . . .' Her vague gesture happened to include the original Degas over the fireplace, the sterling tea service, and even the liveried footman who came in at that moment to clear away.

Mr Lupescu was pretty wonderful that afternoon all right. He had a little kind of an itch like in his wings and they kept twitching all the time. Stardust, he said. It tickles. Got it up in the Milky Way. Friend of his has a wagon route up there.

Mr Lupescu had lots of friends and they all did something you wouldn't ever think of not in a squillion years. That's why he didn't like people because people don't do things you can tell stories about. They just work or keep house or are mothers or something.

But one of Mr Lupescu's friends now was captain of a ship only it went in time and Mr Lupescu took trips with him and came back and told you all about what was happening this very minute five hundred years ago. And another of the friends was a radio engineer only he could tune in on all the kingdoms of faery and Mr Lupescu would squidgle up his red nose and twist it like a dial and make noises like all the kingdoms of faery coming in on the set. And then there was Gorgo only he wasn't a friend, not exactly, not even to Mr Lupescu.

They'd been playing for a couple of weeks only it must've been really hours 'cause Mamselle hadn't yelled about supper yet but Mr Lupescu says Time is funny, when Mr Lupescu screwed up his red eyes and said, 'Bobby, let's go in the house.'

'But there's people in the house and you don't – '

'I know I don't like people. That's why we're going in the house. Come on, Bobby, or I'll – '

So what could you do when you didn't even want to hear him say Gorgo's name?

He went into Father's study through the French window and it was a strict rule that nobody went into Father's study, but rules weren't for Mr Lupescu.

Father was on the telephone telling somebody he'd try to be at a luncheon but there was a committee meeting that same morning but he'd see. While he was talking Mr Lupescu went over to a table and opened a drawer and took something out.

When Father hung up he saw Bobby first and started to be

very mad. He said, 'Young man, you've been trouble enough to your mother and me with all your stories about your red-winged Mr Lupescu, and now if you're to start bursting in – '

You have to be polite and introduce people. 'Father, this is Mr Lupescu. And see he does, too, have red wings.'

Mr Lupescu held out the gun he'd taken from the drawer and shot Father once right through the forehead. It made a little clean hole in front and a big messy hole at the back. Father fell down and was dead.

'Now, Bobby,' Mr Lupescu said, 'a lot of people are going to come here and ask you a lot of questions. And if you don't tell the truth about exactly what happened, I'll send Gorgo to fetch you.'

Then Mr Lupescu was gone through the French window on to the gravel path.

'It's a curious case, Lieutenant,' the medical examiner said. 'It's fortunate I've dabbled a bit in psychiatry; I can at least give you a lead until you get the experts in. The child's statement that his fairy godfather shot his father is obviously a simple flight-mechanism, susceptible of two interpretations. A, the father shot himself; the child was so horrified by the sight that he refused to accept it and invented this explanation. B, the child shot the father, let us say by accident, and shifted the blame to his imaginary scapegoat. B has of course its more sinister implications; if the child had resented his father and created an ideal substitute, he might make the substitute destroy the reality . . . But there's the solution to your eyewitness testimony; which alternative is true, Lieutenant, I leave it up to your researches into motive and the evidence of ballistics and fingerprints. The angle of the wound jibes with either.'

The man with the red nose and eyes and gloves and wings walked down the back lane to the cottage. As soon as he got inside he took off his coat and removed the wings and the mechanism of strings and rubbers that had made them twitch. He laid them on top of the ready pile of kindling and lit the fire. When it was well started, he added the gloves. Then he took off the nose, kneaded the putty until the red of its outside vanished into the neutral brown of the mass, jammed it into a crack in the wall, and smoothed it over. Then he took the red-irised contact lenses out of his brown eyes and went into the kitchen, found a hammer, pounded them to powder, and washed the powder down the sink.

Alan started to pour himself a drink and found, to his pleased surprise, that he didn't especially need one. But he did feel tired. He could lie down and recapitulate it all, from the invention of Mr Lupescu (and Gorgo and the man with the Milky Way route) to today's success and on into the future when Marjorie, pliant, trusting Marjorie would be more desirable than ever as Robert's widow and heir. And Bobby would need a *man* to look after him.

Alan went into the bedroom. Several years passed by in the few seconds it took him to recognise what was waiting on the bed, but then Time is funny.

Alan said nothing.

'Mr Lupescu, I presume?' said Gorgo.

Hobo

Robert Bloch

Hannigan hopped the freight in the yards, just as it started to roll. It had already picked up speed before he spotted an empty in the deepening twilight, and in Hannigan's condition it wasn't easy to swing aboard. He scraped all of the cloth and most of the skin from his left knee before he landed, cursing, in the musty darkness of the boxcar.

He sat there for a moment, trying to catch his wind, feeling the perspiration trickle down under the folds of the dirty jacket. That's what Sneaky Pete did to a man.

Staring out of the doorway, Hannigan watched the lights of the city move past in a blinding blur as the train gained momentum. The lights became links in a solid neon chain. That was also what Sneaky Pete could do to a man.

Hannigan shrugged. Hell, he'd been entitled to drink a few toasts to celebrate leaving town!

Unexpectedly the shrug became a twitch and the twitch became a shiver. So all right, he might as well be honest. He hadn't been celebrating anything. He'd drunk up his last dime because he was scared.

That's why he was on the lam again – he had to get out of Knifeville. That wasn't the name of the town, of course, but Hannigan knew he'd always remember it that way. There wasn't enough Sneaky Pete in the world to drown the memory.

He blinked and turned away from the dwindling chain of light, trying to focus his vision in the dimness of the empty boxcar.

Then he froze.

The boxcar wasn't empty.

Sprawling against the opposite side of the wall was the man. He sat there nonchalantly, staring at Hannigan – and he'd been sitting there and staring all the time. The farther reaches of the car were in total darkness, but the man was just close enough to the opposite door so that flashes of light illumined his features in passing. He was short, squat, his bullet-head almost bald. His face was grimy and stubbled, his clothing soiled and wrinkled. This reassured Hannigan. It couldn't be the Knife.

'Brother, you gave me a scare!' Hannigan muttered. The train was passing over a culvert now and the rumbling cut off the man's reply. When the lights flashed by again he was still staring.

'Going South?' Hannigan called.

The man nodded.

'Me, too.' Hannigan wiped the side of his mouth with his sleeve; he could still taste the Sneaky Pete, still feel it warming his churning guts. 'I don't care where I end up, just so's I get the hell out of that burg.'

They were rolling through open country now and he couldn't see his companion. But he knew he hadn't moved, because now, in counterpoint to the steady clickety-clack of the cars, he heard the steady cadence of his hoarse breathing.

Hannigan didn't give a damn whether he saw him or not – the main thing was just to know he was there, hear the reassuring sound of another man's breath. It helped, and talking helped, too.

'I suppose you hit the iron for the same reason I did.' It was really the Sneaky Pete talking, but Hannigan let the words roll. 'You heard about the Knife?'

He caught the man's nod as a farmhouse light flashed by. The guy was probably drunker than he was, but at least he was listening.

'Damnedest thing. Killed four bums in a week – you see what it said in the papers? Some skull doctor figured it out. This loony just has it in for us poor down-and-outers. I was down in Bronson's jungle yesterday. Half the guys had hit the road already and the rest were leaving. Scared they might be next. I gave 'em all the Bronx salute.'

The stranger didn't reply. Listening to his rasping gasps, Hannigan suddenly realized why. He was blind drunk.

'Loaded, huh?' Hannigan grinned. 'Me, too. On account of I was wrong. About giving those guys the Bronx, I mean.' He gulped. 'Because today – I ran into the Knife.'

The man across the way nodded again; Hannigan caught it in a passing beam of light as the cars rolled on.

'I mean it, man,' he said. 'You know Jerry's place – down the alley off Main? I was crawling out of there this afternoon. Nobody in sight. All of a sudden – zing! Something whizzes right past my ear. I look up and there's this shiv, stuck in a post about three inches from my head.

'I didn't see anyone, and I didn't wait to look. I ducked back into Jerry's and stayed there. Drank up my stake and waited until it was time to hop this rattler.' He was twitching again, but he couldn't help it. 'All I wanted was to get out of there.'

Hannigan leaned forward. 'What's the matter, you a dummy or something?' He tried to catch a glimpse of the man's features, but it was too dark. And now he needed the response. He began to edge forward on his hands and knees as the train lurched over the bumpy roadbed.

'How do you figure it?' he asked – knowing that he was really asking himself the question. 'What gets into a guy's skull that makes him kill that way – just creep around in the dark and carve up poor jokers like us?'

There was no answer, only the hoarse breathing.

Hannigan inched forward, just as the train hit the curve. A light flashed by and he saw the man topple forward.

He saw the blood and the gaping hole and the blinding reflection from the blade of the big knife stuck in the man's back.

'Dead!' Hannigan edged away, shivering, then paused. 'But he can't be. *I heard him breathing!*'

Suddenly he realised he could still hear the breathing now. But it was coming from behind him, coming from close behind. In fact, just as the train went into the tunnel, Hannigan could *feel* the breathing – right against the back of his neck . . .

The Wasteland

Alan Paton

The moment that the bus moved on he knew he was in danger, for by the lights of it he saw the figures of the young men waiting under the tree. That was the thing feared by all, to be waited for by the young men. It was a thing he had talked about, now he was to see it for himself.

It was too late to run after the bus; it went down the dark street like an island of safety in a sea of perils. Though he had known of his danger only for a second, his mouth was already dry, his heart was pounding in his breast, something within him was crying out in protest against the coming event.

His wages were in his purse, he could feel them weighing heavily against his thigh. That was what they wanted from him. Nothing counted against that. His wife could be made a widow, his children made fatherless, nothing counted against that. Mercy was the unknown word.

While he stood there irresolute he heard the young men walking towards him, not only from the side where he had seen them, but from the other also. They did not speak, their intention was unspeakable. The sound of their feet came on the wind to him. The place was well chosen, for behind him was the high wall of the convent, and the barred door that would not open before a man was dead. On the other side of the road was the wasteland, full of wire and iron and the bodies of old cars. It was his only hope, and he moved towards it; as he did so he knew from the whistle that the young men were there too.

His fear was great and instant, and the smell of it went from his body to his nostrils. At that very moment one of them spoke, giving directions. So trapped was he that he was filled suddenly with strength and anger, and he ran towards the wasteland swinging his heavy stick. In the darkness a form loomed up at him, and he swung the stick at it, and heard it give a faint cry of pain. Then he plunged blindly into the wilderness of wire and iron and the bodies of old cars.

Something caught him by the leg, and he brought his stick crashing down on it, but it was no man, only some knife-edged piece of iron. He was sobbing and out of breath, but he pushed on into the waste, while behind him they pushed on also, knocking against the old iron bodies and kicking against tins and buckets. He fell into some grotesque shape of wire; it was barbed and tore at his clothes and flesh. Then it held him, so that it seemed to him that death must be near, and having no other hope, he cried out, 'Help me, help me!' in what should have been a great voice but was voiceless and gasping. He tore at the wire, and it tore at him too, ripping his face and his hands.

Then suddenly he was free. He saw the bus returning, and he cried out again in the great voiceless voice, 'Help me, help me!' Against the lights of it he could plainly see the form of one of the young men. Death was near him, and for a moment he was filled with the injustice of life, that could end thus for one who had always been hard-working and law-abiding. He lifted the heavy stick and brought it down on the head of his pursuer, so that the man crumpled to the ground, moaning and groaning as though life had been unjust to him also.

Then he turned and began to run again, but ran first into the side of an old lorry which sent him reeling. He lay there for a moment expecting the blow that would end him, but even then his wits came back to him, and he turned over twice and was under the lorry. His very entrails seemed to be coming into his mouth, and his lips could taste sweat and blood. His heart was like a wild thing in his breast, and seemed to lift his whole body each time that it beat. He tried to calm it down, thinking it might be heard, and tried to control the noise of his gasping breath, but he could not do either of these things.

Then suddenly against the dark sky he saw two of the young men. He thought they must hear him; but they themselves were gasping like drowned men, and their speech came by fits and starts.

Then one of them said, 'Do you hear?'

They were silent except for their gasping, listening. And he listened also, but could hear nothing but his own exhausted heart.

'I heard a man . . . running . . . on the road,' said one. 'He's got away . . . let's go.'

Then some more of the young men came up, gasping and cursing the man who had got away.

'Freddy,' said one, 'your father's got away.'

But there was no reply.

'Where's Freddy?' one asked.

One said, 'Quiet!' Then he called in a loud voice, 'Freddy.'

But still there was no reply.

'Let's go,' he said.

They moved off slowly and carefully, then one of them stopped.

'We are saved,' he said. 'Here is the man.'

He knelt down on the ground and then fell to cursing.

'There's no money here,' he said.

One of them lit a match, and in the small light of it the man under the lorry saw him fall back.

'It's Freddy,' one said. 'He's dead.'

Then the one who had said 'Quiet' spoke again.

'Lift him up,' he said. 'Put him under the lorry.'

The man under the lorry heard them struggling with the body of the dead young man, and he turned once, twice, deeper into his hiding-place. The young men lifted the body and swung it under the lorry so that it touched him. Then he heard them moving away, not speaking, slowly and quietly, making an occasional sound against some obstruction in the waste.

He turned on his side, so that he would not need to touch the body of the young man. He buried his face in his arms, and said to himself in the idiom of his own language, 'People, arise! The world is dead.' Then he arose himself, and went heavily out of the wasteland.

You Are Now Entering the Human Heart

Janet Frame

I looked at the notice. I wondered if I had time before my train left Philadelphia for Baltimore in one hour. The heart, ceiling-high, occupied one corner of the large exhibition hall, and from wherever you stood in the hall you could hear its beating, *thum-thump-thum-thump*. It was a popular exhibit, and sometimes when there were too many children about, the entrance had to be roped off, as the children loved to race up and down the blood vessels and match their cries to the heart's beating. I could see that the heart had already been punished for the day – the floor of the blood vessel was worn and dusty, the chamber walls were covered with marks, and the notice 'You Are Now Taking the Path of a Blood Cell Through the Human Heart', hung askew. I wanted to see more of the Franklin Institute and the Natural Science Museum across the street, but a journey through the human heart would be fascinating. Did I have time?

Later. First, I would go across the street to the Hall of North America, among the bear and the bison, and catch up on American flora and fauna.

I made my way to the Hall. More children, sitting in rows on canvas chairs. An elementary class from a city school, under the control of an elderly lady teacher. A museum attendant holding a basket, and all eyes gazing at the basket.

'Oh,' I said. 'Is this a private lesson? Is it all right for me to be here?'

The attendant was brisk. 'Surely. We're having a lesson in snake-handling,' he said. 'It's something new. Get the children young and teach them that every snake they meet is not to be killed. People seem to think that every snake has to be knocked on the head. So we're getting them young and teaching them.'

'May I watch?' I said.

'Surely. This is a common grass snake. No harm, no harm at all. Teach the children to learn the feel of them, to lose their fear.'

He turned to the teacher. 'Now, Miss – Mrs – ' he said.

'Miss Aitcheson.'

He lowered his voice. 'The best way to get through to the children is to start with the teacher,' he said to Miss Aitcheson. 'If they see you're not afraid, then they won't be.'

She must be nearing retiring age, I thought. A city woman. Never handled a snake in her life. Her face was pale. She just managed to drag the fear from her eyes to some place in their depths, where it lurked like a dark stain. Surely the attendant and the children noticed?

'It's harmless,' the attendant said. He'd been working with snakes for years.

Miss Aitcheson, I thought again. A city woman born and bred. All snakes were creatures to kill, to be protected from, alike the rattler, the copperhead, king snake, grass snake – venom and victims. Were there not places in the South where you couldn't go into the streets for fear of the rattlesnakes?

Her eyes faced the lighted exit. I saw her fear. The exit light blinked, hooded. The children, none of whom had ever touched a live snake, were sitting hushed, waiting for the drama to begin; one or two looked afraid as the attendant withdrew a green snake about three feet long from the basket and with a swift movement, before the teacher could protest, draped it around her neck and stepped back, admiring and satisfied.

'There,' he said to the class. 'Your teacher has a snake around her neck and she's not afraid.'

Miss Aitcheson stood rigid; she seemed to be holding her breath.

'Teacher's not afraid, are you?' the attendant persisted. He leaned forward, pronouncing judgement on her, while she suddenly jerked her head and lifted her hands in panic to get rid of the snake. Then, seeing the children watching her, she whispered, 'No, I'm not afraid. Of course not.' She looked around her.

'Of course not,' she repeated sharply.

I could see her defeat and helplessness. The attendant seemed unaware, as if his perception had grown a reptilian covering. What did she care for the campaign for the preservation and welfare of copperheads and rattlers and common grass snakes? What did she care about someday walking through the woods or the desert and deciding between killing a snake and setting it free, as if there would be time to decide, when her journey to and from school in downtown Philadelphia held enough danger to occupy her? In two years or so, she'd retire and be in that apartment by herself and no doorman, and everyone knew what happened then, and how she'd be afraid to answer the door and to walk after dark and carry her pocketbook in the street. There was enough to think about without learning to handle and love the snakes, harmless and otherwise, by having them draped around her neck for everyone, including the children – most of all the children – to witness the outbreak of her fear.

'See, Miss Aitcheson's touching the snake. She's not afraid of it at all.'

As everyone watched, she touched the snake. Her fingers recoiled. She touched it again.

'See, she's not afraid. Miss Aitcheson can stand there with a beautiful snake around her neck and touch it and stroke it and not be afraid.'

The faces of the children were full of admiration for the teacher's bravery, and yet there was a cruelly persistent tension; they were waiting, waiting.

'We have to learn to love snakes,' the attendant said. 'Would someone like to come out and stroke teacher's snake?'

Silence.

One shamefaced boy came forward. He stood petrified in front of the teacher.

'Touch it,' the attendant urged. 'It's a friendly snake. Teacher's wearing it around her neck and she's not afraid.'

The boy darted his hand forward, rested it lightly on the snake, and immediately withdrew his hand. Then he ran back to his seat. The children shrieked with glee.

'He's afraid,' someone said. 'He's afraid of the snake.'

The attendant soothed. 'We have to get used to them, you

know. Grownups are not afraid of them, but we can understand that when you're small you might be afraid, and that's why we want you to learn to love them. Isn't that right, Miss Aitcheson? Isn't that right? Now who else is going to be brave enough to touch teacher's snake?'

Two girls came out. They stood hand in hand side by side and stared at the snake and then at Miss Aitcheson.

I wondered when the torture would end. The two little girls did not touch the snake, but they smiled at it and spoke to it and Miss Aitcheson smiled at them and whispered how brave they were.

'Just a minute,' the attendant said. 'There's really no need to be so brave. It's not a question of bravery. The snake is *harmless*, absolutely *harmless*. Where's the bravery when the snake is harmless?'

Suddenly the snake moved around to face Miss Aitcheson and thrust its flat head toward her cheek. She gave a scream, flung up her hands, and tore the snake from her throat and threw it on the floor, and, rushing across the room, she collapsed into a small canvas chair beside the Bear Cabinet and started to cry.

I didn't feel I should watch any longer. Some of the children began to laugh, some to cry. The attendant picked up the snake and nursed it. Miss Aitcheson, recovering, sat helplessly exposed by the small piece of useless torture. It was not her fault she was city-bred, her eyes tried to tell us. She looked at the children, trying in some way to force their admiration and respect; they were shut against her. She was evicted from them and from herself and even from her own fear-infested tomorrow, because she could not promise to love and preserve what she feared. She had nowhere, at that moment, but the small canvas chair by the Bear Cabinet of the Natural Science Museum.

I looked at my watch. If I hurried, I would catch the train from Thirtieth Street. There would be no time to make the journey through the human heart. I hurried out of the museum. It was freezing cold. The icebreakers would be at work on the Delaware and Susquehanna; the mist would have risen by the time I arrived home. Yes, I would just catch the train from Thirtieth Street. The journey through the human heart would have to wait until some other time.